PALEO IN
28

KENZIE SWANHART

PALEO IN 28

4 WEEKS

5 INGREDIENTS

130 RECIPES

FALL RIVER PRESS

New York

To my mother, for teaching me to always
follow my heart and chase my dreams.

FALL RIVER PRESS

New York

An Imprint of Sterling Publishing Co., Inc.
1166 Avenue of the Americas
New York, NY 10036

ISBN 978-1-4351-6752-0

For information about custom editions, special sales, and premium and corporate purchases,
please contact Sterling Special Sales at 800-805-5489 or specialsales@sterlingpublishing.com

Manufactured in China

2 4 6 8 10 9 7 5 3

sterlingpublishing.com

Photo credits: J.R. Photography/ Stocksy. p. 2; Sara Remington/Stocksy, p.6; Sara Remington/Stocksy, p. 8; Jeff Wasserman/
Stocksy, p. 14; Jill Chen/Stocksy, p. 26; Lumina/Stocksy, p. 37; Laura Spinelli/Stocksy, p. 54; Sara Remington/Stocksy, p. 63;
Melanie DeFazio/Stocksy, p. 66; Danny Lerner/Stockfood, p. 73; Sam Stowell/Stockfood, p. 81; Susan Brooks-Dammann/Stocksy,
p. 86; Sarka Babicka/Stockfood, p. 93; Ina Peters/Stocksy, p. 96; Darren Muir/Stocksy, p. 100; Harald Walker/Stocksy, p. 107;
Olga Miltsova/Stockfood, p. 117; Snowflake Studios Inc./Stockfood, p. 120; Noemi Hauser/Stocksy, p. 126; J.R. Photography/
Stocksy, p. 133; Eva Gründemann/Stockfood, p. 141; kkgas/Stocksy, p. 146; Laura Adani/Stocksy, p. 153; Ina Peters/Stocksy, p. 156;
Sean Locke/Stocksy, p. 163; J.R. Photography/Stocksy, p. 166; Stacey Cramp/Stockfood, p. 173; Valerie Janssen/Stockfood, p. 178;
Tim Winter/Stockfood, p. 183; Ralph Lehner Fotografie/Stockfood, p. 188; Jörn Rynio/Stockfood, p. 197; Darren Muir/Stocksy,
p. 204; Glenn Scott/Stockfood, p. 211; Beatrice Peltre/Stockfood, p. 214; Ina Peters/Stocksy, p. 218; és-cuisine/Stockfood, p. 225;
Rua Castilho/Stockfood, p. 232; Gabriel (Gabi) Bucataru/Stocksy, p. 238. All other photos Shutterstock.com.

LET'S GET STARTED

4 weeks. 5 ingredients or fewer.
What do you have to lose?

Whether you are looking to lose weight, improve your health, or achieve a happier lifestyle, following the Paleo diet can help you accomplish your goals. This book will provide you with all the information you need to kick-start your Paleo diet, including a deeper look at the Paleo lifestyle, a 28-day meal plan, and 130 foolproof recipes with five primary ingredients or fewer.

Take a look at the "Paleo Primer" to gain a working knowledge of what it means to eat Paleo. Review the list of foods that you can and cannot eat on the Paleo diet. Then put it all into practice with a four-week meal plan filled with delicious recipes workable for cooks of all levels.

CONTENTS

INTRODUCTION

I discovered Paleo about three years ago, when I was fresh out of college and looking to adopt a healthy lifestyle amidst one of the busiest times of my life. Having just started my first full-time job for a public relations firm in Boston, I was working long hours to learn the ropes, putting in as much overtime as I could. When I wasn't at the office, I was eating out with my boyfriend or grabbing a drink with friends. I was eating high-calorie, high-priced meals at restaurants at night and snacks from the vending machine during the day—not to mention the daily three plus cups of coffee I needed just to stay awake at my desk. Being young and ambitious left me with little time to work out or cook a decent meal.

I was grabbing a cup of coffee at the office one day when a coworker told me about the Paleo diet. She certainly seemed to have her own life pulled together: a blossoming career and enough of a work-life balance to make it to the gym and then home in time to cook a healthy meal every night. One bite of her Paleo breakfast scramble and I was sold. I realized I needed to make a change, and Paleo seemed like the perfect answer.

That night I went home and informed my boyfriend of my grand plans. I told him I wanted to feel good about what I was putting into my body. I wanted to have real energy—not simply live off of caffeine. Most important, I wanted to learn how to cook—to be able to put together a meal from fresh food, not prepackaged or frozen products. Luckily he was on board and supported me every step of the way.

Unfortunately, once I made the decision to adopt the Paleo diet, I discovered there was no central place to go for all the necessary information. So I went into full research mode, buying as many cookbooks as I could carry, looking things up on the Internet until my fingers hurt, and soaking up every piece of information I could about eating Paleo. I probably asked my coworker more than 100 questions while getting started, and she graciously answered each and every one.

A few weeks into my Paleo journey, I decided to start a blog to document my adventures in the kitchen, and *Cave Girl in the City* was born. This little piece of the Internet became the place where I shared my favorite Paleo recipes, described the experience of adopting a Paleo lifestyle, and revealed tips and tricks for staying faithful to Paleo in a modern world. I communicated everything I was learning, and I told my readers the truth about what it was like to begin eating Paleo. Even when my meals were less than true to Paleo guidelines, I felt support from readers and other bloggers. I also enjoyed helping others adopt a healthier, happier lifestyle.

Whether you're going for a drink with friends or hosting a holiday dinner party, I strongly believe that eating Paleo should not impede your ability to live a happy life. After all, taking on the Paleo lifestyle should make you feel good about yourself both inside and out. But, like I said, achieving this goal is easier said than done. The transition to Paleo can be difficult without the right tools and support in getting started.

This is the reason I decided to write *Paleo in 28*—to help others, who are attempting the switch to Paleo, make a smooth transition to this new lifestyle. Not only does this book provide you with all the background knowledge you need to understand exactly what eating Paleo means, but I've designed a four-week meal plan built from recipes with five ingredients or fewer, giving you simple, quick, budget-friendly options easy to work into your busy schedule.

This book will be your best friend for the first four weeks, teaching you valuable lessons you can continually apply as you keep up your Paleo lifestyle. Still can't find what you're looking for, or just need some additional help tackling your first few weeks on Paleo? You can always find me over at *Cave Girl in the City*!

PART I

THE PALEO DIET— A CLOSER LOOK

THE PALEO DIET seems to be taking the world by storm. In fact, in 2013 and 2014, Paleo was named Google's most popular diet among search-engine users. As more people test the Paleo waters and offer their thoughts on the Paleo lifestyle, it is important to understand not only what it means to eat Paleo but also what benefits you can expect to see from adopting this diet of lean meats, vegetables, fruits, and healthy fats.

Here we will take a closer look at the Paleo diet so you can better understand why eating like a caveman (or cave girl) has been scientifically proven to help you lose weight, improve health, and prevent chronic disease.

This fundamental knowledge of what it means to eat Paleo will help you understand which foods you can and cannot eat on a Paleo diet and how to build a well-balanced meal using whole, clean foods. With the help of a few pantry essentials and the Paleo Spice Rack, you will be prepared to tackle the 28-day meal plan and kick off your Paleo lifestyle.

YOUR PALEO PRIMER

Beginning your Paleo journey can appear to be a daunting task without the right tools. But the more you know, the less intimidating this new lifestyle will be. Understanding the principles behind the Paleo diet and how to apply them to your everyday routine will help guide you toward a healthy, balanced lifestyle and simplify your transition to Paleo.

This chapter is a quick Paleo primer meant to provide you with all the background information you need to make well-informed decisions in your first month on the Paleo diet. Whether perusing the aisles of the grocery store or scanning the menu at your favorite restaurant, you will be prepared to make healthy choices that comply with Paleo guidelines.

Let's get started!

WHAT IS PALEO?

You've probably heard the Paleo diet called a lot of things: primal, real food, clean eating, the caveman diet, and hunter-gatherer, among others. Don't let all these names confuse you. Simply put, eating Paleo refers to eating the way our ancestors once did—specifically in the Paleolithic, preagricultural era.

While the exact definition differs from person to person, the underlying principle of eating Paleo remains the same: Eat the foods that make us feel our healthiest. That means ditching the modified, processed, junky foods often consumed in the modern American diet and replacing them with the whole, clean foods we were designed to eat.

Over the past 200,000 years, humans have consumed whole foods packed with the nutrients on which our bodies thrive. It wasn't until recently—in the realm of our evolutionary history, that is—that agriculture came on the scene and we began farming, causing a shift in the American diet. Unfortunately our genetics have not made the same shift, and we have not adapted to eating a grain-rich diet.

Paleo is not a fad diet; it is a lifestyle built on consuming the foods that were meant to fuel our bodies. Instead of relying on high-calorie processed foods such as grains, legumes, dairy, and sugar that have left Americans feeling sick, fat, and unhappy, we need to go back to eating real, whole, unprocessed foods that are more healthful than harmful to our bodies.

The foods eaten by our ancestors mainly consisted of lean meats, vegetables, some fruit, a little bit of starch, and good fats. These are the foods we are genetically wired to consume, which will help us maintain a healthy, active lifestyle.

While all versions of the Paleo diet follow the same premise, it's important to remember that this diet is not one size fits all; nor is there a single list of foods that works best for everyone. Over time, you will discover which foods are optimal for you and your goals. For the purposes of this book and beginning your Paleo journey, stick to a strict Paleo diet for the first 28 days. Once you have mastered the Paleo lifestyle, you can begin to modify and play with the guidelines until you find what works best for you.

THE PROBLEM WITH
THE STANDARD AMERICAN DIET

There is an obvious problem with the Standard American Diet. The way we eat has left Americans feeling unhealthy and out of shape. But why?

- **We have become a species dependent upon processed grains, including bread, pasta, rice, and corn.** In fact, the US government recommends six to eight servings of grains per day. Although grains make up the largest portion of the food pyramid, they actually create the biggest problem with the standard American diet. Grains—especially those containing gluten—are a proven gut irritant, causing digestion issues and inflammation in many Americans.

- **There is a common misconception that high-fat foods make us fat.** Low-fat and nonfat foods are constantly promoted as the healthiest options. This stems from the heavy use of oils devoid of nutrients as ingredients in foods or in food preparation—particularly saturated fats, which are proven to raise your bad cholesterol. In reality, it is sugar that contributes to the expanding American waistline. That being said, it may come as a bit of a surprise that certain dietary fats can be beneficial when consumed properly. These unsaturated fats can even contribute to lowering your cholesterol and your risk of heart disease.

- **Speaking of sugar . . . the average American consumes about 20 teaspoons of sugar a day.** This is more than double the recommended amount, according to the American Heart Association. Different types of sugars have properties that actually produce negative impacts on your brain and other organs—causing hormonal and chemical changes that lead to weight gain.

- **We are a society focused on counting calories.** The problem with this comes when we are consuming low-calorie, overly processed foods. These provide minimal nutritional value—so while you may end up consuming fewer calories than recommended (which seems like a good way to lose weight), you are missing out on vital nutrients necessary for a healthy lifestyle.

Although the Paleo diet may seem restrictive to you at first, keep an open mind and an adventurous palate. Don't be afraid to try new recipes, new foods, and new preparation techniques. Adopting this lifestyle will allow you to taste unfamiliar foods, gain a greater appreciation for the food you eat, and learn more than you ever thought possible about the way food affects your body.

WHAT TO EXPECT

People who adopt a Paleo approach to eating have reported, for some time, significant improvements in their general health, body composition, and energy levels. Personally, over the three-plus years since I have adopted a Paleo lifestyle, I have seen sustained weight loss, increased energy, increased athletic performance, and little-to-no digestion issues.

Due to limited long-term studies and scarce scientific literature on the Paleo lifestyle, the scientific community has been reluctant to provide their support of ancestral nutrition. But as more people embrace this lifestyle, and more data becomes available, several physicians, nutritionists, and other researchers are beginning to tout the benefits of a Paleo diet. Recent studies have proven that the long-claimed benefits of eating Paleo are a reality. By adopting a Paleo lifestyle, you will likely find yourself experiencing:

Increased Weight Loss

One of the most common misconceptions about the Paleo diet is that it is a "fad diet" or quick fix for weight loss, but this is not the case. One reason for this misconception is that when someone removes processed food from their diet and replaces it with whole, clean foods, they often report weight loss in the process of finding their body's optimal health level.

In a new study published in the *European Journal of Clinical Nutrition* titled "Long-term Effects of a Paleolithic-Type Diet in Obese Postmenopausal Women: A 2-Year Randomized Trial," the Paleo diet was shown to increase weight loss at 6, 12, and 18 months and reduce body fat and waist circumference as well as sagittal abdominal diameter at 6 months, as compared to a low-fat, high-carbohydrate diet.

Improved Health

Multiple experimental studies have also proven the Paleo diet to be superior to diabetic diets, Mediterranean diets, and low-fat, high-carbohydrate diets in regard to numerous health factors. In fact, a study in the *Journal of Internal Medicine* demonstrated overall improvements in more than seven important health markers, including blood pressure, total cholesterol, and triglyceride levels. Improvements in various health markers have been seen after just over a week of following the Paleo diet.

Increased Intake of Essential Nutrients

It makes sense that adopting a Paleo lifestyle correlates directly to the increased intake of essential nutrients, given the greater consumption of lean meats, fruits, and vegetables. Eating more meat means absorbing more protein and iron, while a more substantial consumption of vegetables leads to an increase in nutrients and vitamins, such as potassium, dietary fiber, and folic acid.

Note that it is important to make up for a lack of the calcium found in dairy by substituting calcium-rich vegetables, fruits, and nuts, including leafy greens, oranges, figs, and almonds.

Protection Against Chronic Diseases

The increase in daily consumption of fruits and vegetables associated with a Paleo diet also provides anti-inflammatory benefits, which can include protection against chronic diseases.

In addition, a study by Loren Cordain in *The American Nutraceutical Association* journal demonstrated that the nutritional changes accompanying the switch to a Paleo lifestyle can reduce the risk for metabolic syndrome diseases and autoimmunity.

TOSS THE JUNK FOOD

After you've educated yourself about what it means to adopt a Paleo diet, it's time to prepare for this lifestyle change. Most important, you will need to rid your house (pantry, fridge, and secret shelves included) of everything on the "no" list.

Making your house a processed-food-free zone will help you stay on track, even when things get hard. When you get that inevitable sugar craving your first week in, it is so much easier to fall off the wagon when you have a box of cookies hiding in the cabinet rather than a fridge full of fresh apples. You'll thank me later when you don't have to put your willpower to the test. Believe me—it won't win! Here are seven tips for getting your pantry Paleo ready:

1. Fill a big box with all the processed foods in your home, including, but not limited to, all products that include grains, legumes, dairy, and sugar.

2. Separate out any nonperishable items that can be donated, and toss the rest!

3. Once your pantry is clean (pun fully intended), take inventory of everything in your kitchen.

4. Make a note of missing pantry essentials (page 29) and those of which you have multiples.

5. With your list of essentials in hand, hit the store to stock up on the foods that will help you succeed on the Paleo diet—that is, fill your fridge with fresh fruits, vegetables, eggs, meats, and condiments not containing sugar.

6. Keep your pantry free of junk food by sticking to your grocery list and avoiding processed food at the market.

7. Don't forget to organize ingredients within your pantry, including spices, acceptable flours, and other staples, so they are easy to locate. This way, you'll be more apt to use them while cooking.

Increased Energy

Many people cite increased energy as one of the best benefits of adopting a Paleo diet. This increase in energy occurs because foods like lean proteins, high-fiber vegetables, nuts, and healthy oils have a low glycemic index. According to a Harvard Medical School study, this means that sugars from these foods are absorbed more slowly than those in high-carbohydrate foods and refined starches not permitted on the Paleo diet.

Clearer Skin

The food we eat has a direct impact on the way we look and feel. In fact, eating the right foods can prevent the pore blockage, excess oil production, inflammation, and bacterial infection that characterize acne. According to scientist Loren Cordain, by adopting a Paleo diet and eliminating overprocessed, sugar-filled foods, it is possible to improve acne symptoms from the inside out.

7 QUESTIONS EVERY CAVEMAN AND CAVEWOMAN CAN ANSWER

1. How much should I eat on the Paleo diet?

Rather than concentrating on the amount of food you "should" be eating on the Paleo diet, focus on how the foods you eat make you feel. Listen to your body, and eat until you feel full. Although you are not discouraged from eating if you are hungry, it is important to create substantial meals that satisfy you. If you are eating whole, clean foods, you will feel fuller longer, and you'll find that you won't need to worry about grazing in between meals.

2. Doesn't the Paleo diet get boring?

Quite the contrary! One of the biggest challenges in taking on the Paleo diet is being as open as possible to new flavors and foods. There are so many types of meat and vegetables that if you plan ahead and space out what you are cooking, you'll never tire of eating the same dishes over and over again.

WHAT TO EAT AND WHAT NOT TO EAT

Understanding what you can and cannot eat on the Paleo diet is important yet sometimes overlooked. We know that we can eat the way our ancestors did, but what exactly does that mean? At times people get so hung up on the "hunting and gathering" portion of the diet that they don't really think about the actual foods that should and should not be consumed. Remember: Gathering food using agricultural farming techniques is completely different from the foraging done by our ancestors for fruits and vegetables.

The best advice I can give you is this: Eat real food. This includes meat, seafood, eggs, most vegetables and fruits, and good fats from oils, nuts, and seeds. Eat natural, unprocessed foods with very few ingredients (or better yet, no added ingredients at all). When in doubt, read the list of ingredients. If you can't pronounce something, don't eat it. It's as simple as that.

While there are a number of foods to avoid on the Paleo diet, you will be much happier focusing on the foods you can enjoy. Here is a chart to help you navigate these foods. This list is not exhaustive but should be used as a basic guideline.

ENJOY

Fruits
Apples
Apricots
Avocado
Bananas
Berries
Figs
Grapefruit
Guava
Kiwi
Lemons
Limes
Mangos
Melon
Nectarines
Oranges
Peaches
Pears
Pineapple
Plums
Pomegranates
Tangerines
Tomatoes
Watermelon

Healthy Fats
Organic grass-fed butter, ghee
Coconut oil
Lard, tallow
Olive oil

Natural Sweeteners
Agave
Coconut nectar
Maple syrup
Molasses
Raw honey

Nuts and Seeds
Almonds
Brazil nuts
Cashews
Chestnuts
Hazelnuts
Macadamia nuts
Pecans
Pine nuts
Pistachios
Pumpkin seeds
Sesame seeds
Sunflower seeds
Walnuts

AVOID

Alcohol
Cured Meats
Dairy
Fats
Canola oil
Corn oil
Peanut oil

Grains
Barley
Corn
Oats
Quinoa
Rice
Rye
Wheat

Legumes

Protein	Vegetables
Bacon	Artichokes
Beef	Asparagus
Bison	Beets
Chicken	Broccoli
Clams	Brussels sprouts
Cod	Cabbage
Crab	Carrots
Crawfish	Cauliflower
Duck	Celery
Eggs	Cucumbers
Lamb	Eggplant
Lobster	Kale
Mussels	Mushrooms
Octopus	Onions
Oysters	Parsnips
Pork	Peas
Salmon	Pickles
Sardines	Radishes
Scallops	Shallots
Shrimp	Spinach
Squid	Squash
Tilapia	Sprouts
Tuna	Sweet potatoes
Turkey	Tomatoes
Veal	Yams
Venison	Zucchini

Processed Foods

Refined Sugar
Aspartame
Brown sugar
Evaporated cane
Sucralose
White sugar
Other artificial sweeteners

Soy

Is It Paleo Friendly?

Beans: Beans fall under the legume family so are not allowed on the Paleo diet. While legumes are generally considered be a "healthy" food, they contain phytic acid. Because this acid binds to nutrients in food, it prevents you from absorbing them, making legumes nutrient-deficient.

Butter: Butter is a controversial food when it comes to eating Paleo. Organic, grass-fed butter is commonly accepted as Paleo friendly, as it does offer some health benefits and can be a good source of fat when used in moderation. That said, whenever possible, opt for coconut oil, olive oil, or ghee.

Chocolate: Dark chocolate (70 percent or higher), cacao, and carob are types of chocolate generally accepted as Paleo. They come in multiple forms, including chips and powder.

Coffee: Coffee is brewed from roasted coffee beans, which are the seeds of the coffee plant. While coffee is generally acceptable on the Paleo diet, it should be consumed in small quantities, without adding milk or non-Paleo sweeteners. It should not become a crutch for lack of sleep.

Eggs: Don't assume eggs are dairy just because they are found in the grocery store alongside milk, sour cream, and other dairy products. Contrary to popular belief, eggs are embraced on the Paleo diet.

Milk: Cow's milk is not Paleo friendly. Fortunately, almond milk, coconut milk, and others make great substitutes.

Peanuts: Though often mistaken for nuts, peanuts are actually in the legume family and should be avoided.

Potatoes: Potatoes are another controversial topic in the Paleo world. White potatoes are often avoided as they can cause problems for those with digestive sensitivities, while sweet potatoes are widely regarded as Paleo friendly. The recipes in this book use sweet potatoes only, but if you can eat potatoes without digestive issues, feel free to include them in moderation.

Quinoa: Although quinoa is having a "health food moment," it is a grain and should not be consumed on the Paleo diet.

Salt: Adding salt to Paleo foods does not pose a significant health risk, given the substantial amount of salt already cut from one's diet by removing processed food. However, whenever possible, use sea salt instead of table salt.

It is amazing how different combinations of spices can change the entire flavor profile of a dish. One of the greatest things about the diet is that most spices are completely Paleo-approved, so it's easy to get adventurous with flavoring your dishes—guaranteeing you won't get bored of whatever is on your plate.

3. How will I get enough calcium without eating dairy?

The Paleo diet promotes eating a variety of nutrient-dense foods to ensure sufficient intake of vitamins and minerals. Even without eating dairy, it is still possible to get plenty of calcium from Paleo foods, as calcium can be found in a number of nondairy, Paleo-friendly foods such as dark, leafy greens; berries; seafood; and bone broths.

It is always better to get calcium from real food than from supplements, but if you are concerned that you might not be getting enough calcium, you might consider taking a supplement. It's important to note that appropriate calcium intake varies from person to person, so remember to consult your primary care physician before starting any supplement regimen.

4. I am allergic to tree nuts. Is there a good alternative to using almond flour?

A large majority of Paleo recipes and Paleo-friendly baked goods use almond flour, and the recipes you'll find in this book are no exception. I tend to use blanched, finely ground almond flour. For those with nut allergies, finely ground and sifted sunflower seeds are a great substitution.

Coconut flour, on the other hand, cannot be used as an exact substitute for almond flour, as it is more absorbent and requires a different ratio.

Some of my recipes will also call for almond butter. If you are allergic to tree nuts, sunflower seed butter is a good substitution in most cases.

5. Can I dine out on the Paleo diet?

Dining out on the Paleo diet is much easier than it might appear to be; you just have to be vocal about what you want. When you sit down to eat, you may want to let the server know that you do not eat dairy or grains. Don't be afraid to ask how items on the menu are prepared and to ask that your food be cooked with coconut oil, olive oil, or butter. If you are serious about what you can and cannot eat, your server will be too.

6. Is Paleo the same as gluten-free? What is the difference between Paleo and clean eating?

This is similar to the age-old question "Is a square a rectangle, or is a rectangle a square?" The Paleo diet is gluten-free. However, being "gluten-free" does not automatically place you within the Paleo lifestyle. The growing number of people classifying themselves as gluten-free has led to an increasing number of products on the market to meet that need, but many of these are highly processed, containing ingredients that are not Paleo compliant.

"Paleo" and "clean eating" are also not mutually exclusive terms. Throughout this book you will see that I reference the foods you can eat on Paleo as "whole" and "clean." This means that all foods you consume on Paleo should be in their natural state and unprocessed, or as close to this as possible. Those who follow a clean eating plan also eat whole foods, or "real" foods, which are minimally processed, refined, and handled. The biggest difference is that they also eat many foods not considered Paleo, including oats, beans, and peanuts.

7. What makes the Paleo diet different from other diets?

Unlike most diets, the Paleo diet is based on the way we as humans were genetically designed to eat. This is not a trend diet but a sustainable lifestyle promoting a slimmer, happier, healthier you. Instead of a strict, regimented diet focused on helping you lose weight, Paleo is a flexible approach to eating meant to help you feel and look your best.

28 DAYS TO PALEO SUCCESS

Change is always hard, and making a lasting change like adopting a Paleo lifestyle can be intimidating, but now that you know the ropes, you are halfway there. After all, eating Paleo doesn't need to be complicated. Stick to the basics, try new things, and remember to have fun along the way.

You don't need to be a professional chef to prepare a delicious Paleo meal. This meal plan was engineered with the busy person in mind—simple ingredients, short shopping lists, minimal prep, and limited cooking times—all to help you make a successful transition to Paleo.

In this chapter you will learn how to build a balanced Paleo meal using a few pantry essentials, staple spices, and simple kitchen tools.

HOW TO BUILD A PALEO MEAL WITH 5 INGREDIENTS OR FEWER

Growing up, we all learned that a balanced meal consisted of grains, vegetables, fruits, dairy, meat, fats, oils, and sweets. However, now that you understand the principles of the Paleo diet and its benefits, you will need to shift how you envision a balanced meal—and learn how to build a balanced Paleo plate. Unlike traditional "diets," this manner of eating does not demand that you count calories or restrict the quantity of what you consume. Instead, listen to your body and eat when you are hungry. Fill your plate with vegetables, lean meats, some fruit, a little bit of starch, and good fats.

A Balanced Paleo Meal

The building blocks to a well-balanced Paleo meal are simple in concept: eat the whole, clean foods that our ancestors once ate—mainly vegetables, meat, fruit, and good fats. To put this into practice, you just need to know how much of each should fill your plate.

First and foremost, eat a liberal amount of vegetables. Buy fresh, organic vegetables when they are in season, and save money by opting for frozen ones when they aren't. Learn a quick and easy recipe to roast your favorite vegetables, such as Roasted Broccoli (page 159), and look forward to piling them onto your plate!

An appropriate amount of saturated fats is also encouraged. Use saturated fats like coconut oil and grass-fed butter to cook meat and vegetables in place of vegetable oil, canola oil, corn oil, and others. Extra-virgin olive oil can also be used to make salad dressings and condiments.

Eat a moderate amount of animal proteins in the form of grass-fed red meat, poultry, pork, fish, and shellfish. And, lastly, consume a small amount of fruits and nuts. Whenever possible, stick to fruits low in sugar.

All in all, eating Paleo should not be difficult: When in doubt, just remember to fill your plate with vegetables and protein at every meal.

Streamline Ingredients to Save Time and Money

The best thing about cooking with real, unprocessed food is that it is full of flavor—you'll find you don't need to add a lot of extras to produce a delicious meal.

In fact, it's easy to create a wide variety of delicious Paleo meals using five or fewer primary ingredients, a few pantry staples, and simple spices. Pick a meat or vegetable as the base of the meal, and play off of it using other vegetables, saturated fats, herbs, and spices. Remember to keep your recipes simple, and choose a few ingredients that add a lot of flavor. All of the recipes in this book were built using this formula.

Keeping a well-stocked pantry can also help make recipes more streamlined. While I usually recommend using fresh ingredients whenever possible, using dried herbs and spices can help save you time and money. Stocking up on kitchen staples will save you a step during meal prep too, as you won't need to make Paleo basics (like mayonnaise and honey mustard) from scratch.

PANTRY ESSENTIALS

As I mentioned earlier, once you understand the basics of what you can and cannot eat on the Paleo diet, an important next step is to purge your cabinets of the overprocessed food not permitted by Paleo principles. This is important because it is much easier to fall back into old habits with a pantry full of poor food choices.

Rather than viewing this step as negative, think about all the healthy, delicious foods and ingredients you will fill your cabinets with instead. Having a pantry full of Paleo staples will allow you to follow the majority of Paleo recipes you'll find in this book and elsewhere. It will also help you come up with fun, original meal ideas of your own.

Although this list may appear foreign now, once you stock up on these staples, you will feel much more comfortable tackling new recipes.

The list below outlines pantry essentials for every Paleo eater.

Apple cider vinegar
Arrowroot powder
Baking powder
Baking soda
Beef broth, organic
Cacao powder
Chicken broth, organic
Coconut aminos
Coconut, unsweetened shredded
Coconut sugar (coconut crystals)
Dark chocolate chips
Dijon mustard
Dried fruit (apricots, blueberries, cranberries, raisins)
Flour, almond (almond meal)
Flour, coconut

Honey, raw
Hot sauce
Maple syrup
Milk, almond
Milk, coconut
Nuts and seeds (almonds, cashews, pecans, walnuts)
Oil, coconut
Oil, extra-virgin olive
Tomato products, canned (diced, stewed, paste)
Tomato sauce, organic
Vanilla extract
Vegetable broth, organic
White vinegar
Yellow mustard

ALMOND FLOUR VS. ALMOND MEAL

Almond flour is finely ground blanched almonds with the skins removed, while almond meal is ground almonds with the skin still on. Almond meal is much courser than almond flour and is ideal for breading, but it doesn't work as well as blanched almond flour does in baked goods.

THE PALEO SPICE RACK

With an endless list of available spices, eating Paleo should never become boring. That is why no Paleo pantry is complete without a growing spice rack. Whether they have a traditional spice rack that sits out on the counter or a cabinet, drawer, or box full of their favorite spices, every Paleo eater knows the benefit of adding herbs and spices to their recipes. Long gone are the days when your spices collected cobwebs in the back of your cabinet. You will quickly become familiar with each and every one of these spices as they help kick your Paleo dishes up a notch in flavor.

As with the Paleo pantry staples listed earlier, keeping a variety of spices on hand will allow you to follow the majority of Paleo recipes without making continual trips to the store, saving you time, money, and energy down the line.

Below is a list of 25 spices every Paleo cook should have on hand. If you don't already have these spices, you don't need to buy them all at once. Plan to pick up a few each time you go to the market. I also suggest looking for generic, store brands that cost less than the name-brand spices found in the baking aisle. Note that these herbs and spices will not count toward the five ingredients in the recipes in chapters to come.

Allspice

Basil, dried

Bay leaves

Black pepper, freshly ground

Cayenne pepper

Chili powder

Cinnamon

Cloves, ground

Coriander

Crushed red pepper

Cumin

Curry powder

Garlic powder

Garlic salt

Italian seasoning

Mustard, dry

Nutmeg

Onion powder

Onion salt

Oregano, dried

Paprika

Parsley, dried

Rosemary

Sea salt

Thyme, dried

HEALTH BENEFITS OF HERBS AND SPICES

Studies show that in addition to adding flavor to your favorite Paleo dishes, a number of common herbs and spices also offer several health benefits. In fact, some have been shown to possess high levels of antioxidant activity, while others help protect against chronic conditions. Antioxidants present in certain herbs and spices, such as cinnamon, can lower inflammation and reduce blood glucose levels. Other seasonings, such as chili powder, have been linked to a boost in fat-burning capacity.

Get the most from your herbs and spices (both in flavor and health benefits) by storing them in airtight containers away from heat, moisture, and direct sunlight, and using them before their sell-by dates.

KITCHEN TOOLS

Prior to transitioning to the Paleo diet, I had very little experience in the kitchen. Beyond a bowl of cereal or a pot of pasta, I was more of a hazard than a help around dinnertime. Having to learn to cook balanced, healthy meals was one of the most intimidating, yet rewarding, experiences of my Paleo journey.

Here's a secret: You don't need to have a kitchen full of fancy tools to be a good cook. In fact, all you need to get started are the 18 tools below.

Baking sheet
Blender
Cast iron pan
Chef's knife
Cutting board
Food processor
Glass baking dishes
Glass storage containers

Measuring cups

Measuring spoons

Parchment paper

Pots and pans

Rubber spatula

Slow cooker

Stand or hand mixer

Vegetable spiralizer (or julienne peeler)

Whisk

Wooden spoon

DON'T FORGET TO EXERCISE

Eating the foods we are genetically wired to consume is an important factor in maintaining a healthy, active lifestyle, but let's not forget the other key factor at play—exercise. After all, our ancestors didn't just drive to the grocery store to pick up their meat and produce; they didn't even walk to the local farmers' market. Our ancestors hunted and gathered their food. I'm not suggesting that you abandon the modern comforts of your local market and strike out in the wilderness; I am merely maintaining that just as we are genetically wired to eat whole, unprocessed foods, it is also in our nature to be active.

Even if you are eating a clean Paleo diet, you will not achieve the maximum benefit of the Paleo lifestyle without exercise. This might sound like a tall order given everything you need to accomplish in a day, but if you set your mind to it, you'll find it can be surprisingly easy to fit a bit of exercise into your daily routine.

Whether your goal is to lose weight, get stronger, or just lead a healthier life, being active can help get you there. The type of exercise you choose isn't as important as simply taking the time to move your body. Start by prioritizing 10 minutes a day; then choose an activity you enjoy, and do it regularly—it can be as simple as a brisk walk on your lunch break or playing with the kids after dinner. Remember, every little bit makes a difference. Mix it up, keep it interesting, and your workout will feel more like fun than work.

Here are five exercise ideas that are simple to work into a busy schedule.

Go for a Walk

You don't need fancy equipment to get a good workout. Instead, make walking part of your daily routine. If you live in the city and can walk to and from work, make that part of your everyday plan. Even getting off the bus or subway a stop or two early and walking a bit farther than usual is a great way to get in your steps. Don't have the option to commute to work by foot? Find other ways to get moving. Push the baby in a stroller, take the dog for an extra-long walk after dinner, or trade in your tractor for a push mower.

Take a Class

I find that I'm most likely to work out when I am motivated by those around me. That's why I enjoy dedicating about an hour a day to CrossFit. I enjoy the structure of a CrossFit class, the personal attention of the coaches, and the motivation I get from a group of people suffering through a workout-of-the-day (WOD) along with me.

The best part about a class is that you usually have to sign up in advance, and make it a priority to attend, giving you some accountability to show up. There are usually a wide variety of classes offered at a local gym or specialized studio, including boot camp, martial arts, dance, and yoga. Can't commit an hour? Look for classes offered in half-hour and 45-minute increments.

Hit the Gym

Prefer to work out alone? Skip the group workout, and hit the gym instead. There's nothing wrong with a traditional workout, if it's something you love to do. Focus on short, intense sessions instead of spending an hour on the cardio machine. This will allow you to squeeze in a short gym session even on your most hectic of days.

PLAN AHEAD

Preparing Paleo-friendly meals each night can feel like a chore, but 30 minutes of planning on the weekend can help make your nightly meal prep a snap. Try these tips to take the hassle out of cooking.

Organize your kitchen: Keep frequently used cooking tools (such as spatulas, cutting boards, pots, and pans), pantry staples (such as cooking oils and nut flours), and spices, within easy reach. Clean up as you go, and keep your kitchen organized so you always know where everything is.

Plan your meals: Take the guesswork out of your week, and plan your meals in advance. Lining up a week of meals over the weekend will also give you time to purchase ingredients and begin prep. Best of all, you will look forward to cooking rather than agonizing over what to make last minute.

Make a list and go shopping: Once you have planned your meals for the week, make a list of all the ingredients you'll need to pick up. Take inventory of what you already have on hand; then go shopping for the groceries you still need. Having all the ingredients available for a recipe will save a lot of time during the week.

Chop the vegetables: When possible, chop the vegetables you'll need for the week in advance. Do one big prep, and refrigerate all the vegetables in airtight containers. Not only will this save you time down the road, it will also eliminate the need for additional dishes and cleanup.

Make breakfast: I don't need to tell you that breakfast is the most important meal of the day. Unfortunately it is also the one most commonly skipped when you have to prepare it every morning. Instead of waking up early to make eggs, prepare a healthy alternative in advance. See chapter 5 for ideas.

Double the recipe: My favorite trick when preparing meals in advance is to double the recipe. By making an extra batch of food, you'll have enough for lunch the next day, or you can freeze the second batch for another time.

Let Out Your Inner Child

There is something to be said for the way we used to exercise as kids. In fact, I bet you used to have such a good time, you didn't even realize you were exercising. Just because you've grown up doesn't mean exercise can't be entertaining. Make working out a game! Join a local softball team or tennis club, and your workout can be a social activity. A round of golf is also great exercise—just make sure to carry your clubs instead of using a golf cart.

Try Something New

It's important to have fun while being active. Use your daily workout as a way to get outside and try new things. Always wanted to learn to ski? Take a lesson! Experiencing particularly beautiful weather? Get out of the office and take a hike. Looking for something a little daring? Pop in to a rock-climbing gym and throw on a harness.

PART II

28-DAY
MEAL PLAN

WELCOME TO PART II! Now that you understand the basics of the Paleo diet, it's time to put everything you've read into practice. To help you out along the way, I've designed a four-week meal plan, built from recipes with five ingredients or fewer, giving you simple, quick, budget-friendly options that are easy to work into your busy schedule.

Providing three meals a day and offering 10 different snack options to pick and choose from each week, this meal plan takes the guesswork out of cooking. Over the weekend, remember my tips for planning ahead: Take a look at the week of meals to come; review the shopping lists at the end of each week, and see what ingredients you already have on hand; then, go pick up what you need to complete the list.

This meal plan is meant to be flexible, so if a particular recipe doesn't appeal to you one week, you can easily swap it out for another from the 130 recipes in the chapters that follow—they're each built from only five ingredients as well. Just be sure to update your grocery list so that you have everything you need when it comes to meal prep.

The meal plan is also meant to make your life easier. That's why I've incorporated leftovers, make-ahead weekday breakfast options, and weeknight meals that require little prep. The only category not included in the plan is traditional desserts—but that doesn't mean you need to swear off treats for your first 28 days of eating Paleo. Instead, when you feel yourself tempted by the thought of a cookie or cupcake, turn to chapter 11 for something sweet.

Remember that the purpose of this meal plan is to guide you in making the most of your first 28 days, but it is just that—a guide. Should you decide to join friends or family for a meal out, feel confident in the knowledge you gained in the first two chapters about making healthy choices.

I know this all sounds a bit intimidating—I too started from square one. But instead of focusing on all the possible missteps, make a commitment to give Paleo your best effort for 28 days. Write it down or post it on Facebook. Either way, commit to 4 weeks of clean eating on the Paleo diet.

Don't get discouraged if you do experience any setbacks. Shake it off and jump right back on the horse. Remember that this is not an "all or nothing" program. The Paleo diet is all about making the healthiest choices you can.

So, what do you say? Are you ready to eat like a caveman or cavewoman?

3

THE PLAN

WEEK 1

Now that you have rid your kitchen of overprocessed, unhealthy foods, and stocked up on clean, Paleo-friendly foods, it is time to jump feet first into week one of Paleo eating. I'm sure you have experienced a mix of emotions as you prepared for your first week. You were likely excited about eating healthy, delicious foods and the benefits this new lifestyle will have on your body. But it's also possible you experienced anxiety about throwing out some of your favorite junk foods, facing the need to learn to cook (possibly for the first time), and adopting a whole new lifestyle. These feelings are all completely normal.

Your first week on the Paleo diet will very likely be filled with a roller coaster of emotions as you try to become accustomed to a completely new way of looking at food. Your first day or two, you will probably be so motivated about the healthy decisions you're making that you will breeze right through, wondering why you ever thought this was going to be difficult.

The next few days will not be as easy, as your body begins to switch from burning carbohydrates to mainly fat for fuel. This is commonly known as sugar withdrawal. You may experience headaches and fatigue, but this too is completely normal. Just do your best to drink plenty of water and continue to make healthy choices.

As you trek through your first week, it's important to implement the tips and tricks you learned in chapter 1. Remember to plan ahead and prep what you can in advance to make your life a little bit easier. Don't get hung up on the small stuff—just picture the end goal, because you're about to feel amazing!

WEEK 1 MENU

	BREAKFAST	LUNCH	DINNER
SUNDAY	Twice-Baked Breakfast Sweet Potatoes (page 79)	Vegetable Soup (page 113)	Easy Roasted Chicken (page 176) and Roasted Broccoli (page 159)
MONDAY	Baked Egg Cups (page 72)	Leftover Roasted Chicken and Roasted Broccoli	Shrimp Scampi over Zucchini Noodles (page 169)
TUESDAY	Tropical Green Smoothie (page 97)	Cobb Salad (page 105)	Crispy Chicken Tenders (page 181) and Spicy and Sweet Fries (page 157)
WEDNESDAY	Leftover Baked Egg Cups	Pear and Pecan Spinach Salad (page 102)	Baked Spaghetti Bolognese (page 200)
THURSDAY	Strawberry-Banana Smoothie (page 88)	Leftover Baked Spaghetti Bolognese	Pineapple Pulled Pork (page 190)
FRIDAY	Banana Bread Mug Cake (page 85)	Leftover Pineapple Pulled Pork	Chicken Fajitas (page 184) and Cauliflower Rice (page 150)
SATURDAY	Perfect Pancakes (page 80)	Bacon-Cauliflower Soup (page 118)	Chili-Lime Flat Iron Steak (page 195) and Honey-Roasted Sweet Potatoes (page 155)

SNACKS
(CHOOSE ONE OR TWO EACH DAY)

Almonds

Bananas and nut butter

Beef jerky

Cucumber slices

Fried Plantains (page 140)

Grapes

Guacamole (page 132)

Hard-boiled eggs

Mini Pizzas (page 134)

Olives

WEEK 1 SHOPPING LIST

Protein

Bacon, 2 (8-ounce)
packages

Boneless chicken breast
(3 pounds)

Boneless pork shoulder
(2 pounds)

Chicken, whole, 1 (5 pound)

Eggs (2 dozen)

Flat iron steak (2 pounds)

Ground beef (1 pound)

Shrimp, raw (1 pound)

Vegetables

Bell peppers (3)

Broccoli (1 head)

Carrots (3)

Cauliflower (2 heads)

Cherry tomatoes
(1 container)

Garlic (3 heads)

Iceberg lettuce (1 head)

Mushrooms (1 package)

Onions, yellow (4)

Romaine lettuce (1 head)

Shallots (1)

Spaghetti squash, large (1)

Spinach, baby,
2 (10-ounce) bags

Sweet potatoes
(2 pounds plus 4)

Tomato (1)

Yellow squash (1)

Zucchini (4)

Fruits

Avocados (1)

Bananas (5)

Lime (1)

Lemons (6)

Mangos, frozen (1 bag)

Pears (2)

Pineapple (1)

Pineapples, frozen (1 bag)

Strawberries, frozen (1 bag)

Other

Apple juice

Butter, grass-fed

Coconut water

Pomegranate seeds

FROM THE PANTRY

Apple cider vinegar

Arrowroot flour

Baking powder

Basil, dried

Black pepper,
freshly ground

Cayenne pepper

Chicken broth, organic

Chili powder

Cinnamon

Cumin

Flour, almond

Garlic powder

Honey

Milk, almond

Milk, coconut

Mustard, Dijon

Oil, coconut

Oil, extra-virgin olive

Onion powder

Oregano, dried

Paprika

Pecans

Sea salt

Thyme, dried

Tomato sauce, organic

Vanilla extract

White vinegar

WEEK 2

Week one wasn't so bad, was it? I'm sure you had a few sugar cravings, felt less than stellar, and doubted whether you wanted to continue your Paleo journey a few times, but you made it! And if you managed to plan ahead, I'm sure you appreciated it later. If you forgot, let it be a lesson that things are much more pleasant when you prepare in advance.

This week, instead of just buying your food ahead of time, take a minute to portion and prep where you can. Divide your nuts and berries into small containers, so you can grab and go during the week. Prep your morning smoothies by putting all the ingredients in a plastic bag in the freezer; this way no extra work is needed in the morning. Even if you are still struggling to establish your new routine, a few extra minutes of prep the night before can make all the difference the next day.

As you continue to switch from burning carbohydrates (sugar) to fat for fuel, you may experience a few more days of discomfort, headaches, and fatigue. You may also notice your body beginning to change as it adjusts to its new diet. Take solace in knowing this transition period is almost over, and you are about to gain a slimmer waistline, increased energy, and overall better health.

Remember, the more prep work you do in advance, the more prepared you'll be for the challenges you may face in this second week. And you'll soon be moving on to the fun part!

WEEK 2 MENU

	BREAKFAST	LUNCH	DINNER
SUNDAY	Fried Eggs and Diner-Style Sweet Potato Hash (page 82)	Egg Drop Soup (page 122)	Mom's Pot Roast (page 203)
MONDAY	Fried Eggs in a Basket (page 74)	Leftover Pot Roast	30-Minute Beef Chili (page 121)
TUESDAY	Berry Green Smoothie (page 90)	Harvest Vegetable Salad (page 104)	Coconut Shrimp (page 170) and Lemon Zest Grilled Squash (page 164)
WEDNESDAY	Leftover Fried Eggs in a Basket	Simple Egg and Spinach Salad (page 103)	Easy Meatloaf (page 202)
THURSDAY	Almond Butter–Banana Smoothie (page 98)	Apple Walnut Vegetable Salad (page 106)	Slow Cooker Salsa Chicken (page 177) over Cauliflower Rice (page 150)
FRIDAY	Maple Cinnamon Granola (page 68)	Leftover Slow Cooker Salsa Chicken	Spicy Grilled Shrimp Kebabs (page 179) and Roasted Brussels Sprouts with Bacon (page 162)
SATURDAY	Perfect Pancakes (page 80)	Bacon-Cauliflower Soup (page 118)	Fall-Apart Short Ribs (page 192) and Roasted Acorn Squash (page 165)

SNACKS
(CHOOSE ONE OR TWO EACH DAY)

Apples with nut butter

Avocados

Baked Zucchini Chips (page 130)

Berries

Carrot sticks

Coconut yogurt

Deviled Eggs (page 137)

Pineapple-Bacon Bites (page 138)

Pistachios

Raisins

WEEK 2 SHOPPING LIST

Protein

Bacon, 2 (8-ounce)
  packages

Boneless chicken breast
  (2 pounds)

Chuck roast (3 pounds)

Eggs (2 dozen)

Ground beef (3¼ pounds)

Jumbo shrimp (12)

Short ribs (2 pounds)

Shrimp, raw (1 pound)

Vegetable

Acorn squash (1)

Bell pepper (1)

Brussels sprouts (1 pound)

Carrots (3)

Cauliflower (2 heads)

Garlic (2 heads)

Jalepeño (1)

Kale (1 bunch)

Onion, red (1)

Onion, yellow (2)

Purple cabbage (½ pound)

Shallot (1)

Spinach, baby,
  2 (10-ounce) bags

Sweet potatoes (3)

Tomatoes (3)

Yellow squash (6)

Zucchini (4)

Fruits

Apples, honeycrisp (3)

Blueberries, frozen (1 bag)

Bananas (2)

Lemons (5)

Lime (1)

Raspberries, frozen (1 bag)

Fresh Herbs

Basil (1 bunch)

Chives (1 bunch)

Cilantro (1 bunch)

Parsley (1 bunch)

Other

Apple juice

Butter, grass-fed

Red wine

FROM THE
PANTRY

Almond butter

Apple cider vinegar

Baking powder

Basil, dried

Beef broth, organic

Black pepper,
  freshly ground

Cayenne pepper

Cinnamon

Chicken broth, organic

Chili powder

Chipotle chili powder

Coconut, unsweetened
  shredded

Cranberries, dried

Cumin

Flour, almond

Flour, arrowroot

Garlic powder

Ground ginger

Honey

Maple syrup

Milk, almond

Milk, coconut

Mustard, Dijon

Nutmeg

Oil, coconut

Oil, extra-virgin olive

Onion powder

Oregano, dried

Nuts and seeds, raw

Red pepper flakes

Rosemary

Sea salt

Thyme, dried

Tomato paste

Tomatoes, diced

Vanilla extract

Walnuts

WEEK 3

By now you are probably hitting your stride and starting to really enjoy your decision to take on the Paleo diet. Headaches and fatigue should be a thing of the past, as you are hopefully starting to experience some of the positive effects from a diet of lean meats, vegetables, fruits, and healthy fats.

As you continue into week three, you may also be experiencing some chocolate and sugar cravings. Cravings are largely linked to habit, so chances are you're craving something sweet if you are used to having a treat after dinner each night. The cravings won't entirely disappear, but they do become more manageable as you remove processed food from your diet. When you have a craving, chocolate or otherwise, do your best to make healthy choices. The desserts and snacks offered in each week's meal plan can help.

As you are still in the beginning stages of this new diet, any setback—either a conscious choice or an accident—can seem like a very big deal. If you have a small misstep, try your best not to dwell on it. Take a quick inventory of what happened and how you can learn from it, then move on. Remember, each week will get easier as you become increasingly accustomed to living a Paleo lifestyle.

WEEK 3 MENU

	BREAKFAST	LUNCH	DINNER
SUNDAY	Perfect Pancakes (page 80)	Butternut Squash Soup (page 111)	Beef Stew (page 124)
MONDAY	Coconut Porridge (page 69)	Leftover Beef Stew	Pork Chops (page 191) and Mashed Sweet Potatoes (page 154)
TUESDAY	Sunrise Smoothie (page 92)	Simple Egg and Spinach Salad (page103)	Taco and Rice Bowl (page 194)
WEDNESDAY	Quick and Easy Frittata (page 78)	Leftover Taco and Rice Bowl	Sweet Potato Gnocchi (page 172)
THURSDAY	Green Ginger-Peach Smoothie (page 91)	Cobb Salad (page 105)	Stuffed Italian Burgers with Roasted Peppers and Eggplant (page 193)
FRIDAY	Leftover Quick and Easy Frittata	Leftover Stuffed Italian Burgers with Roasted Peppers and Eggplant	Lemon Butter Cod (page 174) and Mashed Cauliflower (page 151)
SATURDAY	N'Oatmeal (page 71)	Creamy Broccoli Soup (page 116)	Chimichurri (page 229) and Family-Style Carrots (page 158)

SNACKS
(CHOOSE ONE OR TWO EACH DAY)

Bacon and avocado

Banana chips

Buffalo Cauliflower Poppers (page 135)

Cashews

Celery sticks and nut or seed butter

Pepper slices and Guacamole (page 132)

Pickles

Pumpkin seeds

Salt and Vinegar Chips (page 128)

Stuffed Mushrooms (page 142)

WEEK 3 SHOPPING LIST

Protein
Bacon (1 package)
Brisket (½ pound)
Cod (1 pound)
Eggs (3 dozen)
Ground beef (3½ pounds)
Pork chops (4)
Stew meat (1 pound)

Vegetables
Broccoli (2 heads)
Butternut squash (1)
Carrots (15)
Cauliflower (3 heads)
Cherry tomatoes
  (1 container)
Eggplant (1)
Garlic (2 heads)
Onions, white (1)
Onion, yellow (1)
Roasted red peppers,
  1 (7-ounce) jar
Romaine lettuce (1 head)
Shallot (1)
Spinach, 2 (10-ounce) bags
Sweet potatoes (7)
Tomato (1)

Fruits
Avocado (1)
Bananas (3)
Lemons (6)
Mangos, frozen (1 bag)
Oranges (2)
Peaches, frozen (1 bag)
Pineapple, frozen (1 bag)

Fresh Herbs
Ginger (1 knob)
Italian parsley (1 bunch)

Other
Butter, grass-fed
Orange juice

FROM THE PANTRY
Apple cider vinegar
Arrowroot powder
Baking powder
Baking soda
Basil, dried
Black pepper,
  freshly ground
Chicken broth, organic
Chili powder

Cinnamon
Coconut, unsweetened
  shredded
Crushed red pepper
Cumin
Dijon mustard
Flaxseed, ground
Flour, almond
Flour, arrowroot
Flour, coconut
Garlic powder
Garlic salt
Honey
Maple syrup
Milk, almond
Milk, coconut
Nutmeg
Oil, coconut
Onion powder
Oregano, dried
Paprika
Parsley, dried
Red wine vinegar
Sea salt
Tomatoes, diced
Vanilla extract

WEEK 4

Congratulations, you have made it to week four, and you've almost reached the end of your first month on the Paleo diet! You are probably thrilled to have come this far, and you may also be a bit anxious about the meal plan ending.

This week you may begin to experience a bit of boredom with the Paleo diet, as you have overcome the biggest obstacles and adapted to a diet of unprocessed, real food. Eating like a caveman/cavewoman is becoming second nature, and while that is fantastic, it is important not to get lazy. Remember that just because you have made it this far, your Paleo journey is not over.

The training wheels may be coming off, and you are now fully equipped to thrive in your new lifestyle, but don't focus on the end of the meal plan; instead, concentrate on week five. Use the knowledge you have gained, your experiences over the past month, and the tools in the upcoming chapters to prepare for the next week. Remember, this is a lifestyle, not a fad diet.

WEEK 4 MENU

	BREAKFAST	LUNCH	DINNER
SUNDAY	Butternut Squash Hash (page 77)	The Easiest Gazpacho (page 109)	Fresh Rosemary Turkey (page 189) with Sautéed Spinach and Mushrooms (page 161)
MONDAY	Baked Avocado Egg Scramble (page 75)	Leftover Fresh Rosemary Turkey with Sautéed Spinach and Mushrooms	Chicken and Broccoli Stir-Fry (page 185)
TUESDAY	Nut Butter Cup Smoothie (page 99)	Leftover Chicken and Broccoli Stir-Fry	Honey-Roasted Salmon (page 182) and Roasted Broccoli (page 159)
WEDNESDAY	Good Morning Mug Biscuits (page 83) and a Fried Egg	Buffalo Chicken Soup (page 123)	Herb Meatballs (page 197) and Tomato Basil Salad (page 152)
THURSDAY	Berry Green Smoothie (page 90)	Italian Wedding Soup (page 115) with leftover Herb Meatballs	Mexican Chicken Burgers (page 180) with Guacamole (page 132)
FRIDAY	Scrambled Egg and Breakfast Sausage (page 84)	Leftover Mexican Chicken Burgers with Guacamole	Simple Scallops (page 171) and Lemon Zest Grilled Squash (page 164)
SATURDAY	Banana Bowl (page 70)	Apple Walnut Vegetable Salad (page 106)	Tangy Tomato Sirloin Tips (page 196)

SNACKS

(CHOOSE ONE OR TWO EACH DAY)

Apple chips

Clementine

Dark chocolate

Mini Burger Sliders (page 145)

Nacho Kale Chips (page 129)

Nuts and berries in coconut milk

Pecans topped with cacao powder

Plantain chips

Taco Dip (page 131)

Unsweetened coconut chips

WEEK 4 SHOPPING LIST

Protein
Bacon (1 package)
Beef sirloin tips (1½ pounds)
Boneless chicken breast
  (2½ pounds)
Eggs (1 dozen)
Ground beef (1 pound)
Ground chicken (2 pounds)
Ground pork (1 pound)
Scallops (2 pounds)
Turkey breast (3 pounds)
Wild salmon fillets (4)

Vegetables
Baby mushrooms
  (½ pound)
Baby spinach,
  2 (10-ounce) bags
Broccoli (2 heads)
Butternut squash (1)
Carrots (3)
Cauliflower (1 head)
Celery (4 stalks)
Cherry tomatoes
  (1 container)
Cucumber (1)
Escarole (1 pound)
Garlic (2 heads)
Iceberg lettuce (1 head)
Jalapeño (1)
Onion, red (1)
Onion, white (1)
Onion, yellow (1)
Purple cabbage (½ pound)

Scallions (1 bunch)
Shallots (2)
Spinach, 2 (10-ounce) bags
Sweet potatoes (7)
Tomatoes (2 pounds plus 5)
Yellow squash (6)

Fruits
Apples, honeycrisp (3)
Avocados (6)
Bananas (4)
Blueberries, frozen (1 bag)
Lemons (4)
Limes (1)
Raspberries, frozen (1 bag)

Fresh Herbs
Basil (1 bunch)
Ginger (1 knob)
Rosemary (1 bunch)

Other
Apple juice
Butter, grass-fed
Red wine

From the Pantry
Almonds
Apple cider vinegar
Baking powder
Basil, dried
Bay leaves
Black pepper,
  freshly ground

Cacao powder
Chicken broth, organic
Chili powder
Cinnamon
Coconut aminos
Coconut, unsweetened
  shredded
Cumin
Dill, dried
Flour, coconut
Garlic powder
Garlic salt
Honey
Hot sauce
Milk, almond
Milk, coconut
Nutmeg
Oil, coconut
Oil, extra-virgin olive
Onion powder
Oregano, dried
Paprika
Parsley, dried
Pecans
Red wine vinegar
Sage
Sea salt
Sesame oil
Sunflower butter
Thyme, dried
Tomato sauce
Walnuts

BEYOND YOUR FIRST 28 DAYS

MAINTAINING A PALEO LIFESTYLE

Now that you have made it through your first month on the Paleo diet, it's time to think about how to maintain this lifestyle moving forward. As we discussed in previous chapters, Paleo is not a trend diet meant to help you lose weight quickly; it is a lifestyle intended to help you be the happiest, healthiest, fittest version of yourself. Following are some tips to help you keep Paleo eating a part of your lifestyle.

Stick with it: My most important tip for someone maintaining a Paleo lifestyle is to stick with it. Maintaining a healthy diet in the modern world is never easy, but the benefits far outweigh all other factors. Many people will feel the urge to give up after one cheat, or a week of particularly poor choices, but it is important to remember why they decided to adopt this diet to start with. Others may get discouraged when they switch to Paleo and it doesn't solve every health problem they have. Remember that diet is only one aspect of living a healthy lifestyle. Stay with it, and begin to assess other areas in your life as well: Are you incorporating exercise into your daily routine, getting enough sleep, and managing stress?

Plan and prep: No matter how long you have been eating Paleo, planning and prepping for the week ahead will always work to your benefit in the long run. Your planning and prep work may shift as you become more comfortable with the Paleo diet and begin experimenting in the kitchen, but the premise will remain the same. Think about the week ahead, make a grocery list, and purchase the food you need. You will also want to do an inventory of your pantry and spice rack every once in a while to avoid running out of the essentials. Perhaps keeping a running list on the fridge will make this easier. The point is to find a system that works best for you and stick to it.

Emergency meals: There will always be days when cooking a healthy, delicious meal just isn't in the cards. Perhaps you have a particularly busy day, or the meal you planned just isn't coming together. That's when emergency meals come in handy. There are two kinds of emergency meals you should always have ready to go. One is a meal you have prepped ahead of time, like my 30-Minute Beef Chili (page 121), and have frozen for the days you just don't have time to cook. The other should be a quick and simple dish you know by heart, have all the ingredients for in your kitchen, and that takes fewer than 15 minutes to prepare.

Keep snacks on hand: Having delicious, healthy snacks within arm's reach will keep you satisfied throughout the day—and your hand out of the cookie jar. Just as you prep meals for the week ahead, it is also important to think about what snacks you like to eat. I like to keep a package of Paleo-friendly trail mix in my purse, a Paleo-approved energy bar in my gym bag, and a drawer full of healthy snacks at my office, so I'm always prepared. If you forget to pack a snack, opt for the banana at your local café instead of a pastry.

Read labels: Lately more and more products boast "gluten-free" and "Paleo" advertisements on their packages, but always read ingredient labels to be sure. Don't take marketing at face value. More than once I have been duped into buying a product containing ingredients that were definitely not Paleo compliant, simply because I trusted what was on the front of a package. The only way to really know if something is Paleo friendly is to read the ingredients and determine for yourself. Remember: If you can't pronounce it, don't eat it.

Order smart: Don't let your diet keep you from spending time with your friends. Dining out on the Paleo diet is actually pretty easy. First off, have a small snack like an apple or veggie sticks before you leave home, so you won't be tempted by the bread basket. Also be sure to check out the restaurant's menu in advance so you can have a plan going in. Opt for a meat or fish entrée with a side of vegetables, and be sure to ask the server to cook your food with coconut oil, olive oil, or butter. Most restaurants are very accommodating, so don't be afraid to ask for what you want, even if it's not listed on the menu.

Share your recipes: Just because your friends don't eat Paleo doesn't mean they won't like the delicious food you prepare for yourself. Invite your friends or family over for a Paleo dinner party, bring a Paleo dish to the next get-together, or bake your coworkers a batch of your favorite Paleo cookies. Pretty soon you'll have everyone asking for your recipes.

Be adventurous: Once a picky eater, I am always amazed at the wide variety of new foods I have discovered over the course of my Paleo journey. Do you love beef? Give bison a try the next time it's on sale at your local market. Missing tortilla chips and guacamole? Why not make some Fried Plantains (page 140) topped with Guacamole (page 132) for an equally delicious snack? Instead of saying no to new foods, promise yourself you will try something at least once before writing it off for good.

Recruit a friend: Adopting a Paleo diet can be quite lonely if you're doing it by yourself. Now that you know the basics, try to recruit a friend. Share your favorite recipes, talk about your experience, and before you know it, someone will be asking to borrow this book! While I have a number of friends who were not interested in adopting the Paleo lifestyle, I now also have a number of coworkers, family members, and friends who eat clean, unprocessed foods like I do.

Drink water: Staying hydrated is important for everyone. Do your best to drink at least eight (8-ounce) glasses of water every day. If plain water gets boring, try adding lemon or lime. You can also opt for carbonated water or seltzer for a little fizz.

ALCOHOL ON THE PALEO DIET

While alcohol is not considered Paleo friendly, it seems unreasonable to think that just because you follow a Paleo lifestyle you are going abstain from drinking and stop going to the bar on Saturday night.

As a general rule, alcohols made from fruit, such as wine and tequila, are generally considered more Paleo friendly than others. Wine is made from fermented grapes, while tequila is made from the agave plant. If you opt for tequila, look for a brand that is 100 percent agave; otherwise, most of what you consume will be sugar.

If you are craving a beer, gluten-free beer or a hard cider are better alternatives, as they don't contain gluten, which may upset your stomach.

Finally, if you opt for hard alcohol, just limit the juices and sugars. Drink it straight, on the rocks, or with a little seltzer to give your drink some fizz.

Ultimately, the key is to watch your body's responses to different alcohols as you start eating Paleo. See how your body reacts, and figure out what works for you.

KEEPING UP YOUR EXERCISE ROUTINE

In order to get the most from your new lifestyle, it's important to make both diet and exercise a priority. If you didn't exercise over the last 28 days, now is a good time to get moving and introduce exercise into your daily routine.

You have already seen the impact eating a Paleo diet can have on your body. Now imagine taking it a step further. Not only will you reap the health benefits of exercise, like improving your immune system, lowering risk of certain diseases, and promoting heart health, but you will also tone your body the way diet alone cannot.

Most important, exercise will keep you strong and fit—both physically and mentally. Getting regular exercise can improve your quality of life by reducing stress and depression, while also improving memory and sleep patterns.

Not sure how to fit exercise into your already busy routine? Go back to chapter 2 to find an activity that you can easily incorporate into your routine; then follow my tips below.

Get up early: Fitting exercise into an already-packed schedule can be tricky, so set your alarm 30 minutes earlier, and get up when it first goes off. Starting your day just half an hour before your regular time will allow you to fit in a spin class or walk to work without disrupting the rest of your day.

Pack your sneakers: Prefer to hit the gym after work? Pack your workout clothes, and take a bag with you to work. You will be much more likely to stop at the gym on your way home if you already have everything you need and don't have to stop home first.

Take a break: Leave a pair of sneakers at the office, and sneak a brisk walk or run in at lunch. Walk around the office park, walk to pick up lunch, or take care of your phone calls while you pace the parking lot. Wearing a pair of comfortable walking shoes will allow you to multitask and get in a bit of exercise.

Make a date: Working out is always more fun with a friend. Instead of meeting up with your friend for a drink after work, why not catch up over a kickboxing class? You can also skip dinner and a movie with your significant other, and hit the ice skating rink or go rock climbing instead!

Reward yourself: It's time to stop thinking of food as a reward. Did you beat your own personal record at the gym? Did you work out every day this month? Reward yourself with new sneakers, an athletic top, or a special yoga class. Find ways to reward yourself in a healthy way, without treating yourself to an extravagant dinner.

Do what you love: You know the saying, "Do what you love, and you'll never work a day in your life"? The same holds true for working out. Pick an activity you enjoy, and your workout will become a pleasure rather than a chore.

TEMPTED BY OLD WAYS

Even the most seasoned Paleo eaters struggle with the Paleo diet at times. It is completely natural to experience sugar cravings, envy your friend's bowl of homemade spaghetti, and want to revert to past eating habits now and then.

When you're tempted to fall back to those old habits, remember how far you have come. Think about the transition period and sugar detox you pulled through to arrive where you are today. If those thoughts aren't enough to deter you from sneaking a cheat meal, here are a few tips and tricks to keep you on track.

Write it down: Use a food diary or smartphone app to log your food throughout the day. Focus on the types of food you are eating rather than counting calories. A piece of candy or slice of bread may not seem like a big deal here or there, but it all adds up. Writing everything down will allow you to keep track and hold yourself accountable to your diet plan.

Buy a cookbook: It's great to have a few go-to meals, but making the same dishes every week can get boring. Jazz up your meal repertoire by testing out some new dishes. Pick up a few new cookbooks, or peruse Paleo blogs for inspiration.

Sub it out: Instead of giving in to your cravings, substitute forbidden foods with delicious, healthy Paleo alternatives. Craving spaghetti and meatballs? Sub the pasta for zucchini noodles or spaghetti squash. Looking for something sweet? Forego the hot-fudge sundae, and make a batch of Paleo Dark Chocolate Pudding (page 208).

Learn how to order in: Whether you're at work late or visiting a friend from out of town, sometimes ordering takeout is inevitable. No matter how much prep work you do, you can't foresee every situation. Don't use inconvenience as an excuse. Instead, be prepared with a few healthy options in your back pocket. I promise you'll be happy you ordered the steak tip salad or burger in a lettuce wrap with sweet potatoes.

Spread the word: Don't be embarrassed to tell your friends and family about your new diet. Educate them as to what you can and can't eat, rather than turning down their dinner party invitations with no explanation. If you do go to a gathering with friends and family, they are more apt to provide a few Paleo-friendly options if they know what's permissible and what isn't—helping you stay on track and far from the mini hot dogs.

MAKE YOUR OWN MEAL PLAN

Just because the 28-day meal plan has ended doesn't mean you should stop planning ahead. As I've stressed throughout this book, success on the Paleo diet is greatly enhanced by your willingness to put in a little prep ahead of time.

Take a few minutes each week to think about your meals for the days ahead, research recipes, and write down a shopping list. Having everything you need for the week to come will make mealtime much less stressful—and leave more time to fit in a walk with the family after dinner.

On the next page you will find a blank one-week meal plan chart to fill out when planning your week. You can also find printable versions of this chart on my blog.

Take a look through the next few chapters, think about the principles of a balanced Paleo plate, and get planning!

YOUR CUSTOMIZED MENU

	BREAKFAST	LUNCH	DINNER
SUNDAY			
MONDAY			
TUESDAY			
WEDNESDAY			
THURSDAY			
FRIDAY			
SATURDAY			

FAVORITE SNACKS
(ONE OR TWO EACH DAY):

PART III

THE RECIPES

I **HAVE CREATED** 130 easy-to-follow recipes, each made with five ingredients and a few pantry essentials to help you as you kick off your Paleo diet. (Essentially, the five ingredients are in addition to common herbs and spices listed in The Paleo Spice Rack [p. 31], cooking fats, and vinegars.) These recipes are staples in my house, and I'm sure they will quickly become favorites in yours as well. Created with your busy lifestyle in mind, the majority of these recipes can be made in 30 minutes or fewer, making them perfect for a weeknight meal. Most of the recipes serve four, but pay attention to the serving size so you can plan your grocery list properly.

As you begin, remember to read through each recipe completely and gather all the ingredients and kitchen tools you will need in advance. As with everything else, a little prep work before you begin to cook will save you time in the long run.

I also suggest that you follow each recipe exactly as written your first time trying it. Then, as you become more comfortable in the kitchen using these ingredients, you can switch things up and play with ingredient selection if you like. Throughout the recipes you will see that I have included helpful tips and suggestions for ingredient substitutes to help you along as you craft your own cooking style. I hope you have as much fun preparing these recipes as I did developing them!

BREAKFAST

Maple Cinnamon Granola

SERVES 6 / SOAK TIME: 24 HOURS / PREP TIME: 20 MINUTES / COOK TIME: 3 HOURS

2 cups mixed raw nuts

Dash sea salt

¾ cup maple syrup

1 tablespoon vanilla

2 tablespoons coconut oil

1 tablespoon cinnamon

½ cup seeds

½ cup dried cranberries

Cooking Tip: *When making any type of granola, it is important to soak the raw nuts to rid them of phytic acid. Soaking raw nuts breaks down the phytic acid so it can be absorbed properly, aiding in digestion. Soaking them also helps the nuts break down into an oat-like consistency.*

IN MENU FOR WEEK:

PER SERVING:
CALORIES 603
TOTAL FAT 38G
SODIUM 69MG
CARBS 57G
SUGARS 38G
PROTEIN 12G

Perfectly crisp, crunchy, and sweet, this recipe is perfect piled atop a scoop of homemade coconut yogurt, in a bowl doused with coconut milk, or simply enjoyed alone as a snack. Granola may take some time to put together, but it can easily be customized based on what you currently have in your pantry. Personally I like to use almonds, walnuts, and sunflower seeds, but you can include whichever nuts and seeds you like best.

1. Put the nuts in a large bowl and cover with water, add a dash of sea salt, and let them soak overnight.

2. Preheat the oven to the lowest setting (about 200°F).

3. Drain the nuts well, and spread them out on a paper towel to dry.

4. In a food processor, grind the soaked nuts until they are coarsely chopped (about the size of granola oats).

5. Add the maple syrup, vanilla, coconut oil, and cinnamon to the food processor, and pulse until well combined.

6. Add the seeds to the food processor, and pulse once or twice.

7. Stir in the dried cranberries.

8. Line 2 baking sheets with parchment paper, and spread the mixture evenly.

9. Bake for 2 to 3 hours and serve.

Coconut Porridge

SERVES 4 / PREP TIME: 5 MINUTES / COOK TIME: 5 MINUTES

Porridge will always taste like pure comfort, so if you tire of eggs easily, this recipe offers a great alternative for a delicious, energy-packed breakfast. Take a minute to enjoy the smooth texture and delicious flavors before tackling your busy day. I find this recipe best when topped with nuts and fresh berries.

1. In a small saucepan, bring the water, maple syrup, coconut milk, coconut flour, and shredded coconut to a boil.

2. Reduce the heat to low and let it simmer for 2 to 3 minutes, stirring halfway through.

3. While the mixture simmers, use a fork to mash the banana in a small bowl.

4. Stir in the mashed banana until thick.

5. Top with the cinnamon and nutmeg and serve.

¼ cup water

1 tablespoon maple syrup

½ cup full-fat coconut milk

3 tablespoons coconut flour

2 tablespoons unsweetened shredded coconut

1 banana

1 teaspoon cinnamon

¼ teaspoon nutmeg

IN MENU FOR WEEK:

PER SERVING:
CALORIES 150
TOTAL FAT 9G
SODIUM 21MG
CARBS 16G
SUGARS 8G
PROTEIN 2G

Banana Bowl

SERVES 1 / PREP TIME: 2 MINUTES / COOK TIME: 30 SECONDS

2 bananas, sliced

¼ cup pecans

2 tablespoons unsweetened shredded coconut

½ cup coconut milk

1 teaspoon cinnamon

IN MENU FOR WEEK:

 4

PER SERVING:
CALORIES 426
TOTAL FAT 21G
SODIUM 15MG
CARBS 62G
SUGARS 31G
PROTEIN 5G

All modern cooks should have a few recipes in their arsenals that don't require an oven or stove. Whether you are pressed for time at home, at the office, or on the road, a healthy breakfast is only 30 seconds away with this quick-and-easy banana bowl.

1. Layer the bananas, pecans, and coconut in a microwave-safe bowl.

2. Top with the coconut milk and cinnamon.

3. Microwave for 30 seconds and serve.

N'Oatmeal

SERVES 1 / PREP TIME: 5 MINUTES / COOK TIME: 10 SECONDS

This recipe is just as satisfying, warm, and creamy as traditional oatmeal—but without the oats. It's perfect for a cold winter morning, and best when topped with a drizzle of maple syrup, shredded coconut, berries, and nuts of your choice.

1. In a small bowl, use a fork to mash the banana.
2. In a medium pan over medium heat, bring the almond milk to a boil.
3. Reduce the heat, and add the egg and egg whites to the almond milk.
4. Once the eggs start to solidify, add the banana, ground flaxseed, and vanilla extract.
5. Stir continuously until thoroughly cooked.
6. Top with cinnamon and nutmeg and serve.

1 banana

½ cup almond milk

1 egg plus 4 egg whites

2 tablespoons
  ground flaxseed

1 teaspoon vanilla extract

1 teaspoon cinnamon

¼ teaspoon nutmeg

IN MENU FOR WEEK:

 3

PER SERVING:
CALORIES 346
TOTAL FAT 11G
SODIUM 290MG
CARBS 35G
SUGARS 17G
PROTEIN 25G

Baked Egg Cups

SERVES 4 / PREP TIME: 5 MINUTES / COOK TIME: 8 MINUTES

Coconut oil, for greasing

4 eggs

4 bacon strips

½ cup fresh spinach

Make-Ahead Tip: *Make a batch of baked egg cups on Sunday night, and enjoy them all week. To reheat, wrap the egg cup with a damp paper towel and microwave for about 15 seconds. Be careful not to overcook them, or your eggs will be rubbery.*

IN MENU FOR WEEK:

PER SERVING:
CALORIES 174
TOTAL FAT 15G
SODIUM 365MG
CARBS 1G
SUGARS 0G
PROTEIN 10G

This recipe has been a staple in our house since my first few weeks of adopting the Paleo diet. Not one for traditional hard-boiled eggs or the egg muffins I often see in other Paleo cookbooks, I was looking for another way to enjoy eggs during the week. This recipe can be made using only eggs for those who prefer to keep the dish simple, or you can add all the meat and veggies you want. Best of all, you can make each and every egg cup a little different, so you eat something new every morning.

1. Preheat the oven to 350°F.
2. Grease a muffin pan with the coconut oil, and crack 1 egg into each muffin cup.
3. Add the bacon and spinach, and scramble the egg mixture with a fork.
4. Cook for about 8 minutes.
5. Remove the muffin tin from the oven when the eggs still look slightly runny and serve.

Fried Eggs in a Basket

SERVES 4 / PREP TIME: 5 MINUTES / COOK TIME: 15 MINUTES

1 bell pepper

Coconut oil, for greasing

4 eggs

Sea salt

**Freshly ground
 black pepper**

IN MENU FOR WEEK:

 2

PER SERVING:
CALORIES 82
TOTAL FAT 6G
SODIUM 121MG
CARBS 2G
SUGARS 2G
PROTEIN 6G

Bright colors and bold flavors collide in this surprisingly easy recipe. You can use a red, yellow, or green bell pepper according to your preference, or use all three for an ultravibrant plate. Sprinkle with salt and pepper, and add a dash of parsley for a little extra flavor.

1. Core and slice the pepper into 4 rings, each about a quarter-inch thick.

2. In a large pan over medium heat, heat the coconut oil.

3. When the pan is hot, place the pepper rings onto the pan.

4. Crack one egg into each ring and cook for about 2 minutes per side.

5. Season with salt and pepper and serve.

Baked Avocado Egg Scramble

SERVES 4 / PREP TIME: 5 MINUTES / COOK TIME: 20 MINUTES

Eggs are a staple in the Paleo diet, but eggs alone can get quite boring. This recipe presents a great way to spice things up and add a bit more healthy fat to your diet. I like to scramble the eggs in this recipe, but it is equally delicious sunny-side up. Not a fan of avocado? Swap it out for hollowed-out tomato or bell pepper with the top cut away and seeds removed.

1. Preheat the oven to 425°F.
2. Scoop out 2 tablespoons of flesh from the center of each avocado.
3. Place the avocados in a small baking dish.
4. Crack 1 egg into each avocado half, using a fork to scramble each egg slightly.
5. Bake for 20 minutes, until the eggs set.
6. Season with salt and pepper and serve.

2 avocados, halved and pitted

4 eggs

Sea salt

Freshly ground black pepper

IN MENU FOR WEEK:

 4

PER SERVING:
CALORIES 268
TOTAL FAT 24G
SODIUM 126MG
CARBS 9G
SUGARS 1G
PROTEIN 8G

Butternut Squash Hash

SERVES 4 / PREP TIME: 10 MINUTES / COOK TIME: 20 MINUTES

Warm apples, fresh squash, and crispy bacon create a comforting, home-cooked hash reminiscent of fall. This recipe is delicious when made with freshly picked apples from the orchard and topped with a fried egg.

1. Heat a large skillet over medium heat and grease using the coconut oil.

2. When the skillet is hot, add the bacon and cook until crispy.

3. Using tongs or a fork, set the bacon aside on a paper towel–lined plate.

4. Add the diced onions to the skillet and cook until translucent. Add the diced butternut squash to the skillet and spread evenly until it starts to brown, about 10 minutes, stirring occasionally.

5. While the butternut squash is cooking, break the bacon into pieces.

6. When the butternut squash is brown (but not burnt), add the apples, and cook until the apples begin to soften.

7. Remove the hash from the stove. Add the bacon, chopped almonds, sea salt, and pepper, and serve.

Coconut oil, for greasing

4 bacon strips

2 cups diced butternut squash

1 cup diced apples

¼ cup chopped almonds

¼ cup diced onions

½ teaspoon sea salt

½ teaspoon freshly ground black pepper

Cooking Tip: *For garnish, add a few sprigs of fresh thyme.*

IN MENU FOR WEEK:

4

PER SERVING:
CALORIES 196
TOTAL FAT 12G
SODIUM 676MG
CARBS 14G
SUGARS 5G
PROTEIN 9G

Quick and Easy Frittata

SERVES 4 / PREP TIME: 5 MINUTES / COOK TIME: 20 MINUTES

4 eggs

2 tablespoons coconut milk

Sea salt

Freshly ground
 black pepper

Coconut oil, for greasing

½ cup cooked brisket
 (or precooked meat of
 your choice)

1 cup spinach (or other
 leftover vegetables)

Cooking Tip: *A cast iron skillet is a great investment because it can be used so many ways. Here I use a skillet because it works equally well on the stovetop and in the oven. You cannot use a regular pan in the oven, because it will warp.*

IN MENU FOR WEEK:

 3

PER SERVING:
CALORIES 169
TOTAL FAT 12G
SODIUM 327MG
CARBS 5G
SUGARS 3G
PROTEIN 10G

One of the easiest ways to make the most of your money is to maximize the potential of your weekly groceries. Don't waste food; instead, think of ways to incorporate scraps into your meals. This recipe is great for using up leftover meat and vegetables at the end of the week. Dice them up, add eggs and coconut milk, and pop it all in the oven: quick, easy, and completely customizable to whatever is left in your fridge.

1. Preheat the oven to 350°F.

2. In a medium bowl, whisk together the eggs and coconut milk, and season with sea salt and pepper.

3. Heat a medium skillet over medium heat, and grease using the coconut oil.

4. When the skillet is hot, add the brisket and spinach leaves, slightly sautéing them.

5. Pour the egg mixture into the skillet, and bake it in the oven for 10 to 15 minutes.

6. Turn up the heat to broil the frittata until cooked through, about 2 minutes, and serve.

Twice-Baked Breakfast Sweet Potatoes

SERVES 4 / PREP TIME: 10 MINUTES / COOK TIME: 1 HOUR, 10 MINUTES

Twice-baked sweet potatoes make a hearty breakfast, but they also provide an excellent side dish when served with chicken. This recipe counts half a sweet potato as one serving. If you are serving this as a stand-alone dish, count a whole potato as one serving.

1. Preheat the oven to 400°F.

2. Poke the sweet potatoes with a fork 4 or 5 times, place directly on the oven rack, and bake for 40 to 45 minutes.

3. In a medium skillet over medium-high heat, fry the bacon until crispy. Do not drain the fat.

4. Remove the bacon from the skillet to a paper towel–lined plate. Add the onion and garlic to the bacon fat. Sauté until the onion is translucent, about 5 minutes.

5. Chop the bacon into ½-inch bits.

6. Once the sweet potatoes have cooled, cut them in half lengthwise, and scoop out the flesh. Reserve the sweet potato skin shells to the side.

7. Add the sweet potato flesh to the skillet, mash to mix with the onion, and cook for 10 more minutes.

8. Season with salt and pepper, and stir in half of the bacon bits.

9. Place the sweet potato skin shells on a parchment paper–lined baking sheet. Scoop the sweet potato mixture into the potato shells and spread evenly.

10. Using the back of a spoon, make a large indentation in the center of the mixture in each potato shell. Crack 1 egg into each indentation, and sprinkle the top with the remaining bacon pieces.

11. Bake the shells for 15 minutes, or until the yoke is set, and serve.

2 sweet potatoes

4 bacon slices

1 yellow onion, diced

4 garlic cloves, minced

Sea salt

Freshly ground black pepper

4 eggs

IN MENU FOR WEEK:

1

PER SERVING:
CALORIES 291
TOTAL FAT 12G
SODIUM 413MG
CARBS 35G
SUGARS 2G
PROTEIN 12G

Perfect Pancakes

SERVES 4 / PREP TIME: 5 MINUTES / COOK TIME: 15 MINUTES

½ cup arrowroot flour

4 tablespoons almond flour

1 teaspoon cinnamon

1 teaspoon baking powder

2 eggs

2 tablespoons coconut milk

Coconut oil, for greasing

Make-Ahead Tip: *Do you miss the convenience of frozen waffles in the morning? Although pancakes don't make for a healthy breakfast every morning, you can enjoy them even if you don't have time to make a fresh batch. Make a batch (or two) in advance and freeze them, then reheat in the toaster oven to achieve a pancake that is crunchy on the outside and soft on the inside.*

IN MENU FOR WEEKS:

   1 2 3

PER SERVING:
CALORIES 90
TOTAL FAT 7G
SODIUM 37MG
CARBS 4G
SUGARS 0G
PROTEIN 4G

I don't make pancakes often, but when I do, I make these. Perfectly fluffy, these pancakes are a special treat on the weekends and for special occasions. Add a handful of blueberries, and top with maple syrup for an extra special treat. If you prefer waffles to pancakes, this batter can also be used in a waffle iron.

1. In a large bowl, stir together the arrowroot flour, almond flour, cinnamon, and baking powder.

2. In a small bowl, whisk together the eggs and coconut milk until well combined.

3. Add the wet ingredients to the dry ingredients, and mix until well combined with no lumps.

4. In a large pan over medium heat, heat the coconut oil.

5. When pan is hot, ladle pancake mix onto the pan and let cook for 2 to 3 minutes per side, or until the pancake begins to bubble.

6. Repeat until all the pancake batter has been used and serve.

Diner-Style Sweet Potato Hash

SERVES 4 / PREP TIME: 10 MINUTES / COOK TIME: 15 MINUTES

2 sweet potatoes, peeled

1 teaspoon garlic powder

1 teaspoon onion powder

1 teaspoon fresh parsley

½ teaspoon sea salt

**½ teaspoon freshly ground
 black pepper**

**1 tablespoon grass-fed
 butter**

Cooking Tip: *Cut your prep
time by using a food pro-
cessor and julienne blade
instead of grating the sweet
potatoes by hand.*

IN MENU FOR WEEK:

 2

PER SERVING:
CALORIES 147
TOTAL FAT 2G
SODIUM 253MG
CARBS 33G
SUGARS 1G
PROTEIN 2G

*Breakfast is one of the easiest meals to eat at a restaurant. Opt
for eggs, skip the toast, and ask for a side of bacon and fruit.
Even though I have it down pat, saying no to diner hash is still
one of the hardest things for me to do. This version of my favorite
shredded and fried hash is made with sweet potatoes, so you can
enjoy this diner favorite without the guilt.*

1. Using a cheese grater, shred the sweet potatoes into a
   large bowl.

2. Add the garlic powder, onion powder, parsley, sea salt,
   and pepper.

3. In a large pan over medium heat, melt the butter.

4. When the pan is hot, add the seasoned sweet potatoes.

5. Toss the sweet potatoes in the pan until they begin
   to brown.

6. Cover with a lid until the sweet potatoes are tender,
   with crispy, brown edges, and serve.

Good Morning Mug Biscuits

SERVES 1 / PREP TIME: 5 MINUTES / COOK TIME: 2 MINUTES

Breakfast sandwiches were always my brother's favorite. In fact, we would often stop at the local deli to pick one up on the way to school. Since most delis don't carry Paleo-friendly bagels and biscuits, this gluten-and-grain-free recipe can help you achieve the same result. Make this recipe in the microwave, and it might just be more convenient than stopping at the deli.

1. In a microwave-safe mug, stir together the coconut flour, baking powder, egg, egg white, butter, almond milk, honey (if using), and salt.

2. Microwave for 2 minutes.

3. Let it cool for 1 minute; then loosen the edge with a knife.

4. Turn the mug over, gently tap on the bottom to free the biscuit, and serve.

1 tablespoon coconut flour

½ teaspoon baking powder

1 egg plus 1 egg white

1 tablespoon grass-fed butter

3 tablespoons almond milk

½ tablespoon honey (optional)

¼ tablespoon sea salt

Serving Tip: *Another delicious way to enjoy these homemade biscuits is to serve them warm with homemade jam.*

IN MENU FOR WEEK:

4

PER SERVING:
CALORIES 289
TOTAL FAT 20G
SODIUM 1555MG
CARBS 18G
SUGARS 12G
PROTEIN 13G

Breakfast Sausage

SERVES 4 TO 6 / PREP TIME: 10 MINUTES / COOK TIME: 20 MINUTES

1 pound ground pork

1 teaspoon dried sage

1 teaspoon dried thyme

1 teaspoon paprika

½ teaspoon nutmeg

½ teaspoon sea salt

½ teaspoon freshly ground black pepper

Make-Ahead Tip: *Make this recipe ahead of time, and freeze. To reheat, add the sausages to a pan, and cook on medium-high heat until warm throughout, about 3 minutes.*

IN MENU FOR WEEK:

PER SERVING:
CALORIES 167
TOTAL FAT 4G
SODIUM 299MG
CARBS 1G
SUGARS 0G
PROTEIN 30G

Homemade sausage is always tastier than the prepackaged version available at your local supermarket, and much easier to prepare than you probably thought. This recipe is the perfect complement to your next omelet, or pile it on top of a Good Morning Mug Biscuit (page 83) with a fried egg.

1. Preheat the oven to 350°F.

2. In a large bowl, use your hands to mix together the ground pork, sage, thyme, paprika, nutmeg, salt, and pepper until well combined.

3. Form the ground pork mixture into equal-size sausage patties or links, and place on a parchment paper–lined baking sheet.

4. Bake for 15 to 20 minutes, or until the center is no longer pink, and serve.

Banana Bread Mug Cake

SERVES 1 / PREP TIME: 5 MINUTES / COOK TIME: 2 MINUTES

I have always had a soft spot for baked goods. Give me the option between eggs and bacon or a slice of banana bread, and my choice will always be the latter. If you're like me and crave something sweet in the morning, this recipe will leave you satisfied without having to devour an entire loaf of sweet bread.

1. In a microwave-safe mug, use a fork to mash the banana.
2. Add the egg, coconut milk, and vanilla extract to the mug, and whisk together with a fork.
3. Add the almond flour, cinnamon, and salt, and mix well.
4. Microwave for 2 minutes and serve.

1 banana

1 egg

2 tablespoons coconut milk

½ teaspoon vanilla extract

2 tablespoons almond flour

½ teaspoon cinnamon

¼ teaspoon sea salt

Cooking Tip: *This recipe is perfect for introducing the kids to the kitchen. You can even let them add a few dark chocolate chips to make it extra indulgent. Looking for a savory switch? Add a small handful of grated zucchini (just be sure to pat dry with a paper towel first).*

IN MENU FOR WEEK:

 1

PER SERVING:
CALORIES 336
TOTAL FAT 19G
SODIUM 536MG
CARBS 33G
SUGARS 17G
PROTEIN 8G

6

SMOOTHIES

Strawberry-Banana Smoothie

SERVES 2 / PREP TIME: 5 MINUTES

¼ cup almond milk

2 bananas

8 frozen strawberries

IN MENU FOR WEEK:

PER SERVING:
CALORIES 199
TOTAL FAT 8G
SODIUM 6MG
CARBS 35G
SUGARS 20G
PROTEIN 2G

Sometimes the most delicious recipes are those with the fewest ingredients. This strawberry-banana smoothie is a classic at our house—we've whipped this one up too many times to count. It's the most convenient recipe since we always have almond milk in the fridge, bananas on the counter, and strawberries in the freezer. Throw it all together in the blender for the perfect breakfast on the go.

In a blender, blend the almond milk, bananas, and strawberries until smooth, 30 to 60 seconds, and serve immediately.

Tropical Berry Smoothie

SERVES 2 / PREP TIME: 5 MINUTES

I love picking my own fruit when the seasons allow. Not only is picking your own food fun, but you get a lot more for your money. In the summer we load up on blackberries, blueberries, raspberries, and strawberries, and freeze enough to last the whole year. The combination of berries and tropical fruit flavors in this smoothie is a refreshing twist on a traditional mixed berry variety.

In a blender, blend the coconut milk, pineapple, raspberries, and strawberries until smooth, 30 to 60 seconds, and serve immediately.

1 cup coconut milk

1 cup frozen pineapple

1 cup frozen raspberries

1 cup frozen strawberries

PER SERVING:
CALORIES 230
TOTAL FAT 3G
SODIUM 9MG
CARBS 54G
SUGARS 44G
PROTEIN 1G

Berry Green Smoothie

SERVES 2 / PREP TIME: 5 MINUTES

½ cup almond milk

1 banana

½ cup frozen blueberries

½ cup frozen raspberries

1 cup baby spinach

Cooking Tip: *If you don't have spinach on hand, replace with another leafy green, such as kale.*

IN MENU FOR WEEKS:

2 4

PER SERVING:
CALORIES 149
TOTAL FAT 1G
SODIUM 58MG
CARBS 36G
SUGARS 25G
PROTEIN 2G

Smoothies are an easy on-the-go meal for a busy lifestyle. If you are the kind of person who wakes up late, you can prepare this recipe in advance by freezing the smoothie in an ice cube tray. Store the smoothie cubes in a freezer-safe plastic bag for effortless preparation in the morning.

In a blender, blend the almond milk, banana, blueberries, raspberries, and spinach until smooth, 30 to 60 seconds, and serve immediately.

Green Ginger-Peach Smoothie

SERVES 2 / PREP TIME: 5 MINUTES

Ginger has long been linked to a number of health benefits, including antioxidant and anti-inflammatory effects. Combine that with the similar health benefits found in spinach, and this recipe is a one-two punch for boosting your immune system— and it's packed with flavor, too.

In a blender, blend the water, peaches, ginger, and spinach until smooth, 30 to 60 seconds, and serve immediately.

1¼ cups water

2 cups frozen peaches

1 teaspoon fresh ginger

1 cup spinach

Cooking Tip: *If you prefer your smoothie a bit sweeter, add 1 tablespoon of honey.*

IN MENU FOR WEEK:

 3

PER SERVING:
CALORIES 73
TOTAL FAT 1G
SODIUM 12MG
CARBS 17G
SUGARS 14G
PROTEIN 2G

Sunrise Smoothie

SERVES 2 / PREP TIME: 5 MINUTES

¼ cup orange juice

1 banana

1 cup fresh or frozen mango

½ cup fresh or frozen pineapple

2 oranges, peeled

Cooking Tip: *If the oranges at the market are less than appealing, pick up tangerines or a grapefruit instead. If you choose to use a grapefruit, you will only need 1 in place of the 2 oranges.*

IN MENU FOR WEEK:

 3

PER SERVING:
CALORIES 226
TOTAL FAT 1G
SODIUM 1MG
CARBS 58
SUGARS 44G
PROTEIN 3G

Packed with vitamin C and bursting with citrus flavor, this recipe is sure to get you moving in the morning. This combination of fruits and juices is aptly named to wake you up and make you smile even on the gloomiest of days. If you use fresh mango and pineapple, throw 4 ice cubes into the blender as well to thicken the smoothie.

In a blender, blend the orange juice, banana, mango, pineapple, and oranges until smooth, 30 to 60 seconds, and serve immediately.

Cranberry-Orange Smoothie

SERVES 2 / PREP TIME: 5 MINUTES

½ cup orange juice

2 bananas

3 ice cubes

4 oranges, peeled

1 cup fresh cranberries

Cooking Tip: *If you find the bananas too overpowering, sub them out for coconut yogurt.*

PER SERVING:
CALORIES 328
TOTAL FAT 1G
SODIUM 3MG
CARBS 82G
SUGARS 56G
PROTEIN 5G

I love the combination of cranberries and oranges; together they offer a refreshing yet warm and comforting embrace. The way they blend in this smoothie is especially delectable—and makes for a delicious breakfast on the go.

In a blender, blend the orange juice, bananas, ice cubes, oranges, and cranberries until smooth, 30 to 60 seconds, and serve immediately.

Pumpkin Spice Smoothie

SERVES 2 / PREP TIME: 5 MINUTES

Pumpkin spice–flavored beverages can be enjoyed year round, even if they aren't always given center stage at your local coffee shop until November. Tame your pumpkin craving or save some money by whipping up your own pumpkin spice drinks. This pumpkin spice smoothie is refreshing enough for the warmer months but still offers the warm, bold flavors of your favorite fall beverages.

In a blender, blend the almond milk, pumpkin purée, maple syrup, cinnamon, nutmeg, cloves, and ice until smooth, 30 to 60 seconds, and serve immediately.

½ cup almond milk

¼ cup organic
  pumpkin purée

1 tablespoon maple syrup

¼ teaspoon cinnamon

¼ teaspoon nutmeg

¼ teaspoon cloves

1 cup ice

Cooking Tip: *If the smoothie is too thick for your preference, add a bit more almond milk to thin it out. Prefer it thicker? Add more ice.*

PER SERVING:
CALORIES 49
TOTAL FAT 1G
SODIUM 49MG
CARBS 10G
SUGARS 7G
PROTEIN 1G

Tropical Green Smoothie

SERVES 2 / PREP TIME: 5 MINUTES

Packed with nutrient-dense superfoods and vitamin-filled fruits, this healthy concoction is disguised as a delicious tropical drink. Fresh fruits and coconut water lend their tropical flavors to completely conceal the taste of spinach. Whip one up for breakfast or an afternoon snack, and the energy boost will keep you moving throughout the day.

In a blender, blend the coconut water, bananas, mango, pineapple, and spinach until smooth, 30 to 60 seconds, and serve immediately.

1 cup coconut water

2 bananas

1 cup frozen mango

1 cup frozen pineapple

2 cups spinach

Cooking Tip: *Replace the coconut water with coconut milk for a richer smoothie.*

IN MENU FOR WEEK:

 1

PER SERVING:
CALORIES 242
TOTAL FAT 1G
SODIUM 37MG
CARBS 62G
SUGARS 45G
PROTEIN 3G

Almond Butter–Banana Smoothie

SERVES 2 / PREP TIME: 5 MINUTES

1 cup almond milk

4 or 5 ice cubes

1 banana

1 tablespoon almond butter

IN MENU FOR WEEK:

PER SERVING:
CALORIES 118
TOTAL FAT 6G
SODIUM 91MG
CARBS 15G
SUGARS 7G
PROTEIN 3G

This recipe is my all-time favorite and my go-to when I need a midday snack at work. I keep an inexpensive single-serve blender at the office, almond milk in the fridge, and nut butter in my desk drawer. Bring a banana with you in the morning (or a few each week), and you have everything you need for a quick and healthy afternoon treat.

1. In a blender, blend the almond milk, ice cubes, banana, and almond butter until smooth, 30 to 60 seconds, scraping down the sides of the blender if needed.

2. Serve immediately.

Nut Butter Cup Smoothie

SERVES 2 / PREP TIME: 5 MINUTES

This decadent recipe is a frozen treat best enjoyed on special occasions or when you're craving something sweet. Bursting with rich flavors, this smoothie tastes more like a peanut butter and chocolate milkshake than a Paleo-friendly breakfast.

1. In a blender, blend the almond milk, banana, honey, sunflower butter, and cacao powder until smooth, 30 to 60 seconds, scraping down the sides of the blender if needed.

2. Serve immediately.

¾ cup almond milk

1 frozen banana

1 tablespoon honey

1 tablespoon sunflower butter

3 tablespoons cacao powder

IN MENU FOR WEEK:

4

PER SERVING:
CALORIES 161
TOTAL FAT 6G
SODIUM 69MG
CARBS 29G
SUGARS 16G
PROTEIN 4G

SALADS, SOUPS, AND STEWS

Pear and Pecan Spinach Salad

SERVES 2 TO 4 / PREP TIME: 10 MINUTES

2 pears

6 cups baby spinach

⅓ cup pomegranate seeds

½ cup pecans

**Spiced Cider Vinaigrette
  (page 227)**

Make-Ahead Tip: *Prepare
the salad in advance without the pears and salad
dressing and chill. Add the
pears and salad dressing
just before serving.*

IN MENU FOR WEEK:

PER SERVING (SALAD ONLY):
CALORIES 240
TOTAL FAT 6G
SODIUM 74MG
CARBS 48G
SUGARS 27G
PROTEIN 5G

*Using my foolproof salad-making technique, combining greens,
fruit, and nuts, I added pears, pecans, and pomegranate seeds
to put a colorful, fruity spin with a dash of crunch on this spinach
salad. If pears aren't in season, replace them with apples or
another seasonal fruit. You can also sub out the pecans for
sliced almonds.*

1. Core and slice the pears into ⅛-inch-thick slices.

2. In a large bowl, toss the spinach, pears, pomegranate
    seeds, and pecans.

3. Drizzle with Spiced Cider Vinaigrette and serve.

Simple Egg and Spinach Salad

SERVES 2 TO 4 / PREP TIME: 10 MINUTES

Topped with hard-boiled eggs and crunchy bacon, this salad is much more filling than its four ingredients would let on. If you're looking to make this the main event, simply add cooked chicken for extra protein.

1. In a large bowl, toss the spinach, eggs, and bacon.
2. Drizzle with Simple Lemon Dressing and serve.

1 (10-ounce) bag fresh spinach

6 eggs, hard boiled and sliced

8 bacon slices, cooked and chopped

Simple Lemon Dressing (page 226)

Cooking Tip: *For perfectly hard-boiled eggs, place eggs in a single layer at the bottom of a pot. Cover with cold water, exceeding the height of the eggs by 1 inch. Bring the water to a boil, and then remove the pot from the heat. Let it stand for 12 minutes.*

IN MENU FOR WEEKS:

 2 3

PER SERVING (SALAD ONLY):
CALORIES 542
TOTAL FAT 42G
SODIUM 1421MG
CARBS 6G
SUGARS 2G
PROTEIN 37G

Harvest Vegetable Salad

SERVES 2 TO 4 / PREP TIME: 30 MINUTES / COOK TIME: 30 MINUTES

4 cups kale

4 tablespoons extra-virgin
  olive oil, divided

Sea salt

Freshly ground
  black pepper

1 sweet potato, chopped

1 teaspoon cinnamon

1 apple, chopped

½ cup chopped walnuts

Spiced Cider Vinaigrette
  (page 227)

IN MENU FOR WEEK:

 2

PER SERVING (SALAD ONLY):
CALORIES 601
TOTAL FAT 47G
SODIUM 197MG
CARBS 42G
SUGARS 14G
PROTEIN 13G

Contrary to its name, this salad recipe can be enjoyed year round. Hearty vegetables, fresh fruit, and earthy kale evoke a feeling of fall, but these tasty ingredients can be found at the market throughout the year.

1. Preheat the oven to 400°F.

2. In a large bowl, combine the kale and 2 tablespoons of olive oil, and season with salt and pepper. Toss well and massage the kale for 2 minutes. Spread the kale on a parchment paper–lined baking sheet, and bake for 15 minutes, tossing halfway through.

3. Remove from the oven and set aside.

4. In a small bowl, mix together the sweet potato, remaining 2 tablespoons of olive oil, and cinnamon until well combined. Spread the sweet potato mixture on a parchment paper–lined baking sheet, and bake for 15 to 20 minutes.

5. Remove from the oven, add the apples and walnuts, toss, and bake for another 15 minutes.

6. In a large bowl, toss the kale, sweet potatoes, apples, and walnuts.

7. Drizzle with Spiced Cider Vinaigrette and serve.

Cobb Salad

SERVES 4 TO 6 / PREP TIME: 20 MINUTES

The neatly arranged, colorful rows of a Cobb salad make it both beautiful to look at and delicious to eat. Piled with protein, fresh fruit, and vegetables, this salad is a hearty meal and a welcomed party dish.

1. Fill a large bowl with romaine lettuce.
2. Arrange the eggs, bacon, avocado, and cherry tomatoes on top of one another in neat rows.
3. Drizzle with Simple Lemon Dressing and serve.

1 head romaine
  lettuce, chopped

6 eggs, hard-boiled
  and sliced

8 bacon slices, cooked
  and chopped

1 avocado, diced

1 cup cherry tomatoes,
  chopped

Simple Lemon Dressing
  (page 226)

IN MENU FOR WEEKS:

 1 3

PER SERVING:
CALORIES 422
TOTAL FAT 33G
SODIUM 980MG
CARBS 10G
SUGARS 3G
PROTEIN 24G

Apple Walnut Vegetable Salad

SERVES 2 TO 4 / PREP TIME: 10 MINUTES

**1½ cup shredded
   purple cabbage**

⅓ cup shredded carrots

2 honeycrisp apples, diced

½ cup chopped walnuts

**Spiced Cider Vinaigrette
   (page 227)**

Cooking Tip: *Add chives for
a little extra color.*

IN MENU FOR WEEKS:

PER SERVING (SALAD ONLY):
CALORIES 329
TOTAL FAT 19G
SODIUM 33MG
CARBS 38G
SUGARS 26G
PROTEIN 9G

*A small salad topped with seasonal fruit, crunchy nuts, and a
simple salad dressing is a great way to start your meal. It also
makes for an easy lunch or dinner—just add a pile of chicken!*

1. In a large bowl, toss the shredded cabbage and carrots.

2. Top with diced apples and chopped walnuts.

3. Drizzle with Spiced Cider Vinaigrette and serve.

Cold Strawberry Soup

SERVES 4 / PREP TIME: 10 MINUTES

4 cups fresh strawberries

1 cup freshly squeezed orange juice

2 cups full-fat coconut milk

3 teaspoons vanilla extract

Toasted coconut flakes, for garnish (optional)

PER SERVING:
CALORIES 323
TOTAL FAT 25G
SODIUM 32MG
CARBS 22G
SUGARS 15G
PROTEIN 3G

This creamy strawberry purée offers a change from your typical bowl of hot, steamy soup. It's especially refreshing in summer when the mercury just keeps rising. Try it as a starter dish or even dessert.

1. Using a small knife, remove the leafy stems from the top of each strawberry.

2. In a blender, blend the strawberries, orange juice, coconut milk, and vanilla extract until completely smooth.

3. Garnish with coconut flakes (if using) and serve chilled.

The Easiest Gazpacho

SERVES 6 / PREP TIME: 10 MINUTES

Like the Cold Strawberry Soup on page 108, this gazpacho is served chilled. Although cold soup may sound like a misnomer, I promise this one is a real treat. Gazpacho is another refreshing, flavorful dish perfect for a hot summer day.

1. In a blender, pulse the tomatoes 4 or 5 times.
2. Add the cucumber, shallot, garlic, and red wine vinegar. Blend on a medium speed or "blend" setting.
3. While the blender is running, slowly add in the olive oil to mix it evenly into the soup.
4. Once the ingredients are fully combined, season with salt and pepper.
5. Serve chilled.

2 pounds tomatoes, chopped

1 cucumber, peeled and chopped

1 shallot, peeled and chopped

2 garlic cloves, minced

2 tablespoons red wine vinegar

¼ cup extra-virgin olive oil

Sea salt

Freshly ground black pepper

IN MENU FOR WEEK:

4

PER SERVING:
CALORIES 110
TOTAL FAT 9G
SODIUM 48MG
CARBS 8G
SUGARS 5G
PROTEIN 2G

Butternut Squash Soup

SERVES 4 / PREP TIME: 10 MINUTES / COOK TIME: 1 HOUR 20 MINUTES

In addition to being delicious, butternut squash is an excellent source of vitamins A and C. Roasting the vegetables gives this creamy soup a robust flavor profile that is sure to have you asking for seconds.

1. Preheat the oven to 350°F.

2. Halve the butternut squash lengthwise. Use a large spoon to scoop the seeds out of the inside.

3. Line a baking sheet with aluminum foil, and place the squash halves face down. Roast for 60 minutes.

4. In a large pot over low heat, melt the butter.

5. Allow the squash to cool for a few minutes; then scoop out the cooked squash from the skins into the pot.

6. Add ½ cup of chicken stock to the squash.

7. Using a potato masher, mash the squash until there are no more lumps. Scoop down the sides of the pot multiple times to ensure you are incorporating all of the squash.

8. Add the remaining ½ cup of chicken stock and the garlic powder, season with salt and pepper, and stir well to combine.

9. Cook for an additional 10 minutes, and serve hot.

1 butternut squash

2 tablespoons grass-fed butter

1 cup chicken stock, divided

½ teaspoon garlic powder

Sea salt

Freshly ground black pepper

Cooking Tip: *Spice things up by adding roasted pears or apples in with the butternut squash. These fruits both complement the flavor of the soup.*

IN MENU FOR WEEK:

3

PER SERVING:
CALORIES 116
TOTAL FAT 2G
SODIUM 274MG
CARBS 25G
SUGARS 5G
PROTEIN 3G

Onion Soup

SERVES 4 / PREP TIME: 10 MINUTES / COOK TIME: 1 HOUR

4 tablespoons grass-fed
  butter

1 tablespoon coconut oil

2 white onions, sliced

3 yellow onions, sliced

4 cups beef stock

3 cups chicken stock

Sea salt

Freshly ground
  black pepper

PER SERVING:
CALORIES 144
TOTAL FAT 9G
SODIUM 1451MG
CARBS 14G
SUGARS 7G
PROTEIN 6G

The bold flavors of beef and onion come together beautifully in this rich, melt-in-your-mouth soup. Just be sure to skip the cheese and croutons traditionally served on top. You may be surprised at just how little you'll miss them.

1. In a large pot over medium-low heat, melt the butter and coconut oil.

2. Add the white and yellow onions to the pot, stirring continuously.

3. Turn the heat up to medium, and allow the onions to begin to caramelize. The color should be an opaque white—not clear.

4. Add the beef stock and chicken stock, and cook until the soup is simmering.

5. Stir regularly, and season with salt and pepper.

6. Continue to cook so the soup can reduce. The soup is ready to serve when it has reduced by half—after about 1 hour.

Vegetable Soup

SERVES 4 / PREP TIME: 10 MINUTES / COOK TIME: 1 HOUR

This vegetable soup is full of hearty, fresh vegetables that are delicious and nutritious—so go ahead; fill up on this childhood favorite guilt free. It's perfectly filling alone, or you can try it with hot, steamy Good Morning Mug Biscuits (page 83).

1. In a large pot over medium heat, melt the butter.
2. Put the onion, carrots, yellow squash, and mushrooms in the pot.
3. Add the chicken stock, cumin, thyme, and basil, and season with salt and pepper.
4. Stir well to combine.
5. Cover the pot, and turn the heat down to low.
6. Cook for 1 hour and serve.

1 tablespoon grass-fed butter

1 yellow onion, coarsely chopped

3 carrots, coarsely chopped

1 yellow squash, coarsely chopped

1½ cups coarsely chopped mushrooms

3 cups chicken stock

¾ teaspoon cumin

1 teaspoon dried thyme

2 teaspoons dried basil

Sea salt

Freshly ground black pepper

IN MENU FOR WEEK:

 1

PER SERVING:
CALORIES 62
TOTAL FAT 2G
SODIUM 679MG
CARBS 11G
SUGARS 6G
PROTEIN 3G

Home-Cooked Chicken Soup

SERVES 6 / PREP TIME: 10 MINUTES / COOK TIME: 7 HOURS

1 white onion, chopped

3 celery stalks, diced

3 carrots, diced

1 teaspoon apple cider vinegar

1 tablespoon Herbes de Provence

1 pound boneless chicken breast

1 teaspoon sea salt

½ teaspoon freshly ground black pepper

3 to 4 cups water

PER SERVING:
CALORIES 219
TOTAL FAT 4G
SODIUM 642MG
CARBS 8G
SUGARS 4G
PROTEIN 37G

Tender chicken, fresh vegetables, and the most flavorful broth make this chicken soup recipe a favorite—a comfort when you're feeling under the weather or simply on a cold winter day. Herbes de Provence and apple cider vinegar bring out new depths of flavor in this classic dish.

1. In a slow cooker, layer the onion, the celery, and then the carrots.
2. Add the apple cider vinegar and Herbes de Provence.
3. Place the chicken in a single layer on top of the vegetables.
4. Add the salt and pepper to the top of the chicken.
5. Slowly pour the water into the slow cooker.
6. Cook on low for 7 hours.
7. When you are ready to eat, remove the chicken from the slow cooker, and shred it with two forks. Add the chicken back into the soup, stir to combine, and serve.

Italian Wedding Soup

SERVES 6 / PREP TIME: 15 MINUTES / COOK TIME: 20 MINUTES

This hearty soup is filled with an array of colorful greens, fresh vegetables, and herb meatballs. It's so good that the term "wedding soup" actually refers to how well the greens and meats go together. This dish is perfect on a cold night—or any night of the year.

1. In a large pot over medium-high heat, bring the chicken broth to a boil.

2. Add the escarole and carrots (if using), and cook until tender, about 7 minutes.

3. In a small bowl, whisk the eggs.

4. Stir the soup in a clockwise motion. While the soup is moving, slowly pour in the eggs.

5. Use a fork to continue the clockwise stirring motion. The egg will form into thin strands of cooked egg.

6. Season with salt and pepper, and add the meatballs.

7. Cook for an additional 10 minutes and serve.

6 cups chicken broth

1 pound escarole, coarsely chopped

1 cup finely chopped carrots (optional)

2 eggs

Sea salt

Freshly ground black pepper

Herb Meatballs (page 197)

IN MENU FOR WEEK:

 4

PER SERVING:
CALORIES 316
TOTAL FAT 15G
SODIUM 987MG
CARBS 9G
SUGARS 3G
PROTEIN 37G

Creamy Broccoli Soup

SERVES 6 / PREP TIME: 10 MINUTES / COOK TIME: 1 HOUR 15 MINUTES

2 heads broccoli, coarsely chopped

1 head cauliflower, coarsely chopped

1 white onion, chopped

4 cups chicken broth

1 cup full-fat coconut milk

1 tablespoon grass-fed butter

Sea salt

Freshly ground black pepper

IN MENU FOR WEEK:

 3

PER SERVING:
CALORIES 174
TOTAL FAT 10G
SODIUM 581MG
CARBS 14G
SUGARS 5G
PROTEIN 8G

One of my all-time favorite soups to eat at a restaurant used to be broccoli and cheddar. This one is so easy to make at home—and so enjoyable you won't even miss the dairy.

1. In a large pot over high heat, bring the broccoli, cauliflower, onion, chicken broth, coconut milk, and butter to a boil. Reduce the heat to low, and cook for 30 minutes.

2. Season with salt and pepper, and allow the soup to cool for 30 minutes.

3. Fill a blender pitcher with the soup to the marked maximum height, and blend on high until the consistency is smooth. Empty into a large bowl or different pot. Repeat until all the soup is blended. Alternatively, use an immersion blender to blend the soup while still warm.

4. Reheat on the stove until warm and serve.

Bacon-Cauliflower Soup

SERVES 6 / PREP TIME: 10 MINUTES / COOK TIME: 1 HOUR

5 bacon slices, chopped

1 onion, chopped

½ teaspoon garlic powder

1 head cauliflower

3 cups organic chicken broth

⅓ cup coconut milk

1 teaspoon sea salt

1 teaspoon freshly ground black pepper

Cooking Tip: *If you love to make soups, a great kitchen tool to consider adding to your collection is an immersion blender. This stick-shaped blender can be inserted into liquids, hot or cold, to blend them. If you have an immersion blender for this recipe, you don't have to wait for the soup to cool before blending.*

IN MENU FOR WEEKS:

PER SERVING:
CALORIES 159
TOTAL FAT 11G
SODIUM 1076MG
CARBS 6G
SUGARS 3G
PROTEIN 10G

Creamy and delicious, this cauliflower soup radiates bacon in every bite. It's the perfect indulgence when you crave a comforting dish. The rich flavor is sure to make you forget that it's dairy-free.

1. In a large pot over medium heat, brown the bacon for 10 minutes. Remove the bacon to a paper towel–lined plate, keeping the bacon fat in the pot.

2. Add the onion and garlic powder to the bacon fat, and sauté until the onion is soft.

3. Cut the head of cauliflower into small florets, and add them to the pot.

4. Turn the heat to high, and add the chicken broth.

5. Once the broth is boiling, add the bacon, cover the pot, and turn the heat to low.

6. After 10 minutes, add the coconut milk, stir, and remove the pot from the heat.

7. Add the salt and pepper, and allow the soup to cool for 30 minutes.

8. Fill a blender pitcher with the soup to the marked maximum height, and blend on high until the consistency is smooth. Empty into a large bowl or different pot. Repeat until all the soup is blended.

9. Reheat on the stove until warm and serve.

Tomato Herb Soup

SERVES 4 / PREP TIME: 5 MINUTES / COOK TIME: 1 HOUR 15 MINUTES

If you love tomatoes, you will love this soup. Tangy yet creamy, this recipe is perfect for when you're craving that garden fresh tomato taste in something warm. It is also a nice bonus that tomatoes are bursting with lycopene and vitamin C.

1. In a large pot over high heat, bring the crushed tomatoes, tomato paste, chicken broth, basil, coconut milk, and butter to a boil. Reduce the heat to low, and cook for 30 minutes.

2. Season the soup with salt and pepper, and allow it to cool for 30 minutes.

3. Fill a blender pitcher with the soup to the marked maximum height, and blend on high until the consistency is smooth. Empty into a large bowl or different pot. Repeat until all the soup is blended. Alternatively, use an immersion blender to blend the soup while still warm.

4. Reheat on the stove until warm and serve.

2 (28-ounce) cans crushed tomatoes

1 (6-ounce) can tomato paste

3 cups chicken broth

½ cup fresh basil

1 cup full-fat coconut milk

4 tablespoons grass-fed butter

Sea salt

Freshly ground black pepper

PER SERVING:
CALORIES 379
TOTAL FAT 17G
SODIUM 1482MG
CARBS 43G
SUGARS 30G
PROTEIN 17G

30-Minute Beef Chili

SERVES 4 / PREP TIME: 5 MINUTES / COOK TIME: 25 MINUTES

Chili is usually a pretty big production in our house. We spend all day making a big batch, and then have leftovers for at least a week. But what about those times you're looking for a hearty bowl of chili and don't have hours to spend in the kitchen? This recipe has the full, bold flavor of a pot of home-cooked chili, but is ready in just 30 minutes.

1. In a large pan over medium heat, heat the olive oil and brown the garlic.
2. Add the ground beef to the pan and brown.
3. Add the chili powder, chipotle chili powder, onion powder, oregano, and cumin, and season with salt and pepper. Stir well.
4. Add the tomatoes, let simmer for 25 minutes, and serve.

2 tablespoon extra-virgin olive oil

4 garlic cloves, minced

1¼ pounds ground beef

3½ tablespoons chili powder

1 teaspoon chipotle chili powder

2 teaspoons onion powder

2 teaspoons dried oregano

2 teaspoons cumin

Sea salt

Freshly ground black pepper

1 (8-ounce) can diced tomatoes

Cooking Tip: *Bake a batch of Spicy and Sweet Fries (page 157), and top them with this chili recipe for a quick game-day snack.*

IN MENU FOR WEEK:

 2

PER SERVING:
CALORIES 371
TOTAL FAT 18G
SODIUM 230MG
CARBS 9G
SUGARS 3G
PROTEIN 45G

Egg Drop Soup

SERVES 4 / PREP TIME: 5 MINUTES / COOK TIME: 10 MINUTES

3 cups chicken stock

¼ teaspoon ground ginger

¼ teaspoon sea salt

¼ teaspoon dried thyme

¼ teaspoon freshly ground black pepper

2 tablespoons chives, coarsely chopped

2 eggs

IN MENU FOR WEEK:

2

PER SERVING:
CALORIES 40
TOTAL FAT 3G
SODIUM 721MG
CARBS 1G
SUGARS 1G
PROTEIN 3G

One of those takeout classics, egg drop soup can easily be replicated at home. This recipe is so easy—I'll bet you have all the ingredients in your pantry and refrigerator at all times.

1. In a medium pot over high heat, heat the chicken stock, ginger, salt, thyme, pepper, and chives.
2. In a small bowl, whisk the eggs.
3. Bring the pot to a boil.
4. Slowly pour the whisked eggs into the pot while slowly stirring the liquid.
5. Cook the soup for 10 minutes.
6. Serve immediately.

Buffalo Chicken Soup

SERVES 4 / PREP TIME: 15 MINUTES / COOK TIME: 35 MINUTES

My boyfriend is obsessed with Buffalo chicken—wings or tenders during the big game are an absolute must for him. As a healthier (and less messy) option, I made him this soup, and he couldn't get enough of it.

1. In a large pot over high heat, stir the cauliflower, chicken stock, water, dill, and garlic powder together.

2. Boil for 10 minutes.

3. While the cauliflower is boiling, melt the butter in a medium pan over medium heat. Add the onion powder and celery, and cook until the celery is tender, about 5 minutes.

4. Remove the cauliflower from the heat, and using a potato masher, mash the cauliflower until there are no lumps. Stir regularly and scrape down the sides of the pot to fully combine all ingredients.

5. Add the hot sauce and sautéed celery to the pot, and stir to combine.

6. Put the chicken in the pot and stir.

7. Turn the heat to low, and simmer for 25 minutes.

8. Serve immediately.

1 head cauliflower, coarsely chopped

3 cups chicken stock

¾ cup water

2 teaspoons dried dill

1 teaspoon garlic powder

1 tablespoon grass-fed butter

1 teaspoon onion powder

4 stalks celery, chopped

¾ cup hot sauce

1½ pounds boneless chicken breasts, cooked and shredded

IN MENU FOR WEEK:

 4

PER SERVING:
CALORIES 369
TOTAL FAT 14G
SODIUM 1905MG
CARBS 7G
SUGARS 4G
PROTEIN 52G

Beef Stew

SERVES 4 / PREP TIME: 10 MINUTES / COOK TIME: 5 TO 8 HOURS

1 pound stew meat, cut into
  1-inch cubes

1 sweet potato, chopped

3 carrots, chopped

1 (14½-ounce) can
  diced tomatoes

1½ cups chicken stock

1 teaspoon apple
  cider vinegar

1 teaspoon dried basil

1 teaspoon dried oregano

1 teaspoon onion powder

½ teaspoon cumin

Sea salt

Freshly ground
  black pepper

Beef stew just spells "comfort food" in my book. I always used to request my grandma's home-cooked stew growing up, and this recipe reminds me of home. The sweet potato puts a delicious Paleo spin on a classic.

1. Place the stew meat, sweet potato, and carrots on the bottom of a slow cooker.

2. Add the diced tomatoes, chicken stock, apple cider vinegar, basil, oregano, onion powder, and cumin to the slow cooker, and season with salt and pepper. Stir to combine all the ingredients.

3. Cook on high for 5 hours, or on low for 8 hours, and serve.

IN MENU FOR WEEK:

 3

PER SERVING:
CALORIES 356
TOTAL FAT 15G
SODIUM 473MG
CARBS 16G
SUGARS 7G
PROTEIN 38G

Chicken Chili

SERVES 4 / PREP TIME: 5 MINUTES / COOK TIME: 35 MINUTES

When most people think of chili, they immediately expect beef. Try changing it up with this version featuring shredded chicken and green chiles for a new twist on an old favorite.

1. In a large pot over medium heat, heat the chicken, tomatoes, tomato sauce, green chiles, chicken stock, chili powder, basil, cumin, garlic powder, and oregano, and season with cayenne pepper.

2. Once the chili comes to a boil, turn the heat down to low.

3. Cover the pot, simmer for 30 minutes, and serve.

1 pound boneless chicken breast, cooked and shredded

1 (14½-ounce) can diced tomatoes

1 (8-ounce) can tomato sauce

1 (4-ounce) can diced green chiles

½ cup chicken stock

1 tablespoon chili powder

2 teaspoons dried basil

2 teaspoons cumin

1½ teaspoons garlic powder

1 teaspoon dried oregano

Cayenne pepper, for seasoning

PER SERVING:
CALORIES 244
TOTAL FAT 5G
SODIUM 663MG
CARBS 11G
SUGARS 7G
PROTEIN 39G

8

SNACKS

Salt and Vinegar Chips

SERVES 4 / PREP TIME: 15 MINUTES / COOK TIME: 30 MINUTES

3 sweet potatoes

⅓ cup malt vinegar

3 teaspoons sea salt

Coconut oil, for greasing

Cooking Tip: *Use a sharp knife or a mandolin to slice the sweet potatoes into very thin discs.*

If you do not have a wire rack, place the sweet potatoes directly on nonstick aluminum foil. Just be sure to coat thoroughly with coconut oil.

IN MENU FOR WEEK:

 3

PER SERVING:
CALORIES 270
TOTAL FAT 0G
SODIUM 1425MG
CARBS 63G
SUGARS 1G
PROTEIN 3G

Salt and vinegar potato chips are one of those snacks you just can't put down. This version adds a bit of unexpected sweetness to balance out the strong flavor profile.

1. Preheat the oven to 375°F.
2. Slice the sweet potatoes into thin, round discs.
3. Add the sweet potatoes, malt vinegar, and salt to a gallon-size plastic bag.
4. Close the bag and shake until the sweet potatoes are well coated. Let stand for 10 minutes.
5. Line a baking sheet with parchment paper, and place a wire rack on top. Coat generously with coconut oil.
6. Place the sweet potatoes in a single layer on the wire rack.
7. Bake for 30 to 40 minutes, flipping halfway through.
8. Remove, allow to cool completely, and serve.

Nacho Kale Chips

SERVES 4 / PREP TIME: 15 MINUTES / COOK TIME: 5 HOURS

Kale chips are a snacking staple for many Paleo eaters. Quick and easy, oil and sea salt are usually my go-to seasonings, but sometimes this can get a bit boring—so I like to mix these up with other fun flavors, like nacho or ranch.

1. Preheat the oven to 170°F.
2. Tear the kale into bite-size pieces, and set aside on a paper towel to dry.
3. In a food processor, blend the sunflower seed butter, coconut oil, chili powder, cumin, garlic powder, salt, and pepper, scraping down the sides as needed.
4. Add the kale and the sunflower seed butter mixture to a gallon-size plastic bag, and toss until the kale is well coated.
5. Spread out the kale in a single layer on a parchment paper–lined baking sheet.
6. Bake in the oven until the chips are dry and crispy, about 5 hours.
7. Cool and serve.

2 bunches kale, washed and stemmed

2½ tablespoons sunflower seed butter

1 tablespoon coconut oil

¾ teaspoon chili powder

½ teaspoon cumin

½ teaspoon garlic powder

½ teaspoon sea salt

¼ teaspoon freshly ground black pepper

Cooking Tip: *Store kale chips in an airtight container to keep them crispy. If they get a bit tender, you can briefly pop them back in the oven.*

IN MENU FOR WEEK:

4

PER SERVING:
CALORIES 190
TOTAL FAT 8G
SODIUM 327MG
CARBS 24G
SUGAR 0G
PROTEIN 8G

Baked Zucchini Chips

SERVES 6 TO 8 / PREP TIME: 15 MINUTES / COOK TIME: 1 HOUR

4 zucchini

Coconut oil, for greasing

Paprika, for sprinkling

**Chipotle chili powder,
 for sprinkling**

Sea salt

Cooking Tip: *Use a sharp
knife or a mandolin to
slice the zucchini into very
thin discs.*

*If you don't have a wire
rack, place the zucchini
directly on nonstick alu-
minum foil. Just be sure
to coat thoroughly with
coconut oil.*

IN MENU FOR WEEK:

 2

PER SERVING:
CALORIES 41
TOTAL FAT 3G
SODIUM 52MG
CARBS 4G
SUGARS 2G
PROTEIN 2G

*Vegetable chips are a great alternative to the overprocessed
potato chips that line supermarket aisles. And just as store-
bought chips come in a diverse range, you can make a number of
different vegetable chips in a variety of flavors. Follow this recipe,
but switch up the spices to try new flavor combinations.*

1. Preheat the oven to 250°F.

2. Slice the zucchini into thin, round discs.

3. Line a baking sheet with parchment paper, and place a
   wire rack on top. Coat generously with coconut oil.

4. Place the zucchini in a single layer on the wire rack.
   Sprinkle with paprika, chipotle chili powder, and salt.

5. Bake for 1 hour, or until golden brown.

6. Cool and serve.

Taco Dip

SERVES 4 TO 6 / PREP TIME: 10 MINUTES / COOK TIME: 12 MINUTES

Layer after layer of delicious, fresh ingredients make this recipe one of my favorite appetizers to offer at a summer barbecue or football party. Serve with a pile of salty plantain chips, and everyone will rave about your amazing hosting skills.

1. In a pan over medium-high heat, cook the ground beef until brown.

2. Add the Taco Seasoning and water, and let the meat simmer for 4 to 5 minutes.

3. While the beef is simmering, shred the lettuce into small pieces.

4. Drain the beef, as needed.

5. Layer the beef, Guacamole, Salsa, lettuce, and olives (if using) in a serving dish and serve.

1 pound ground beef

2½ tablespoons Taco Seasoning (page 221)

½ cup water

1½ cups chopped iceberg lettuce

2 cups Guacamole (page 132)

2 cups fresh Salsa (page 236)

1 cup black olives, sliced (optional)

Cooking Tip: *To save time, you can purchase premade guacamole and salsa at your local market. Look for fresh guacamole and salsa in the refrigerated section, and be sure to read all ingredients for Paleo compliance.*

IN MENU FOR WEEK:

4

PER SERVING:
CALORIES 541
TOTAL FAT 32G
SODIUM 1838MG
CARBS 25G
SUGARS 5G
PROTEIN 41G

Guacamole

SERVES 4 TO 6 / PREP TIME: 15 MINUTES

¼ red onion, minced

½ teaspoon sea salt

Juice of 1 lime

4 avocados, halved
  and pitted

1 jalapeño, diced

½ tomato, chopped

Garlic salt, for seasoning

Freshly ground
  black pepper

Cooking Tip: *Adding the salt and lime juice to the onion first allows it to precook. If you prefer raw onion, just add it in with everything else.*

IN MENU FOR WEEKS:

PER SERVING:
CALORIES 459
TOTAL FAT 39G
SODIUM 251MG
CARBS 29G
SUGARS 6G
PROTEIN 5G

I put guacamole on just about everything, and although it is one of my favorite condiments, it also makes a delicious snack when served with Fried Plantains (page 140) or veggie sticks.

1. In a large bowl, stir together the onion, salt, and lime juice, and let sit for 5 to 10 minutes.

2. Score the avocado into small sections, and use a spoon to scoop out the fruit along the edge of the skin.

3. Add the avocado, jalapeño, and tomato to the bowl, and season with garlic salt and pepper.

4. Mix everything together, using a potato masher to reach desired consistency.

Mini Pizzas

SERVES 4 TO 6 / PREP TIME: 10 MINUTES / COOK TIME: 10 MINUTES

4 zucchini

2 tablespoons extra-virgin
  olive oil

Sea salt

Freshly ground
  black pepper

⅓ cup tomato sauce

½ cup mini pepperoni slices

Dried oregano

Cooking Tip: *If you can't find mini pepperoni slices at your local market, pick up regular pepperoni slices, and chop them into smaller pieces that fit on the zucchini discs.*

IN MENU FOR WEEK:

PER SERVING:
CALORIES 237
TOTAL FAT 20G
SODIUM 667MG
CARBS 8G
SUGARS 4G
PROTEIN 9G

This recipe is not only a healthier option than those mini pizza bagels you used to eat as a kid, but these Mini Pizzas are sure to impress your guests as well. Make a batch for your next party or for a quick and easy weekend snack. Get creative and add your favorite pizza toppings, like sausage, pineapple, and onions.

1. Preheat the oven to the broil setting.

2. Slice the zucchini into ¼-inch-thick discs.

3. In a pan over medium-high heat, heat the olive oil.

4. Place one layer of zucchini discs in the pan, and cook for 2 minutes per side. Season with salt and pepper.

5. Place the zucchini discs on a parchment paper–lined baking sheet.

6. Top each zucchini disc with tomato sauce, pepperoni, and dried oregano.

7. Bake for 1 to 2 minutes and serve.

Buffalo Cauliflower Poppers

SERVES 4 / PREP TIME: 10 MINUTES / COOK TIME: 20 MINUTES

These hot and spicy Buffalo Cauliflower Poppers are a great alternative to the breaded chicken wings that so often dominate the tables of family barbecues and game-day tailgates. Serve with a side of Ranch Dressing (page 223), and enjoy guilt free.

1 head cauliflower

2 tablespoons extra-virgin olive oil

½ teaspoon sea salt

½ teaspoon freshly ground black pepper

3 tablespoons buffalo or hot sauce

1. Preheat the oven to 450°F.

2. Chop the cauliflower into florets.

3. Add the cauliflower, olive oil, salt, and pepper to a gallon-size plastic bag. Toss until the cauliflower is well coated.

4. Place the seasoned cauliflower on a parchment paper–lined baking sheet.

5. Bake for 15 minutes, flipping halfway through.

6. In a large bowl, toss the cauliflower with the buffalo or hot sauce.

7. Arrange the coated cauliflower on the lined baking sheet, bake for an additional 5 minutes, and serve.

Cooking Tip: *When baking the cauliflower, continue to check on its tenderness so that the cauliflower is crispy, not mushy.*

IN MENU FOR WEEK:

 3

PER SERVING:
CALORIES 78
TOTAL FAT 7G
SODIUM 539MG
CARBS 4G
SUGARS 2G
PROTEIN 1G

Deviled Eggs

SERVES 4 / PREP TIME: 20 MINUTES / COOK TIME: 15 MINUTES

Deviled eggs are a quick snack you can easily make Paleo friendly. Prep them in advance and store in an airtight container so you can nibble on them throughout the week.

1. In a large pot, place the eggs in a single layer at the bottom. Add cold water to cover the eggs by 1 inch.

2. Bring the water to a boil; then remove the pot from the heat. Let it stand for 12 minutes.

3. Rinse the eggs under cold water continuously for 1 minute.

4. Carefully remove the shells from the eggs, and pat dry with a paper towel.

5. Halve the eggs lengthwise, and gently remove the yolks. Put the yolks in a medium bowl, and place the egg whites on a serving dish.

6. Use a fork to mash the yolks. Add Mayonnaise, avocado, mustard, and salt, and season with pepper. Mix well.

7. Place a tablespoon of the yolk mixture back into each of the egg whites.

8. Sprinkle with paprika and serve.

8 eggs

¼ cup Mayonnaise (page 230)

½ avocado

1 tablespoon yellow mustard

⅛ teaspoon sea salt

Freshly ground black pepper

Paprika, for garnish

IN MENU FOR WEEK:

 2

PER SERVING:
CALORIES 237
TOTAL FAT 19G
SODIUM 332MG
CARBS 7G
SUGARS 2G
PROTEIN 12G

Pineapple-Bacon Bites

SERVES 6 / PREP TIME: 15 MINUTES / COOK TIME: 30 MINUTES

12 strips bacon

½ pineapple, skin removed

Cooking Tip: *The bacon should be cold when wrapping the pineapple. The warmer the bacon, the more difficult it is to handle.*

IN MENU FOR WEEK:

PER SERVING:
CALORIES 219
TOTAL FAT 16G
SODIUM 878MG
CARBS 4G
SUGARS 3G
PROTEIN 14G

If you've been missing the combination of pineapple and bacon in your life, these little bites are here to fill the void. Perfectly crisp on the outside and juicy on the inside, these scrumptious nibbles will have you head over heels in no time. I'll bet you can't have just one!

1. Preheat the oven to 425°F.

2. Halve the bacon strips width-wise.

3. Dice the pineapple into ¾-inch cubes.

4. Wrap each pineapple chunk in a half-strip of bacon, securing with a toothpick where the bacon overlaps.

5. Place on a parchment paper–lined baking sheet, and bake for 25 to 30 minutes, or until crispy, and serve.

Baby BLT Bites

SERVES 2 TO 4 / PREP TIME: 10 MINUTES / COOK TIME: 5 MINUTES

Growing up, BLTs were a household favorite for a quick and easy lunch. In this recipe I tossed the bread and gave the traditional BLT a little makeover. All you need to do is pile the ingredients on a toothpick, and you have a delicious (and adorable) Paleo-friendly snack.

1. In a medium pan over medium-high heat, fry the bacon until cooked but not crispy.

2. Using tongs or a fork, remove the bacon from the pan to on a paper towel–lined plate to drain excess oil.

3. Chop each slice of bacon into four pieces.

4. Chop the lettuce.

5. Put two pieces of bacon, two pieces of lettuce, and one cherry tomato on each toothpick and serve.

4 strips bacon

3 leaves romaine lettuce

8 cherry tomatoes

Cooking Tip: *Cook the bacon thoroughly, but not overly so—if it's too crispy, you won't be able to poke a toothpick through it.*

PER SERVING:
CALORIES 295
TOTAL FAT 17G
SODIUM 902MG
CARBS 20G
SUGARS 13G
PROTEIN 18G

Fried Plantains

SERVES 2 / PREP TIME: 5 MINUTES / COOK TIME: 15 MINUTES

2 green plantains

4 tablespoons coconut oil

Sea salt

Cooking Tip: *The term "green plantain" doesn't refer to the color—it indicates the variety of plantain. Be sure to choose ripe plantains. They should be a dull yellow color with patches of black.*

IN MENU FOR WEEK:

PER SERVING:
CALORIES 453
TOTAL FAT 28G
SODIUM 124MG
CARBS 57G
SUGARS 27G
PROTEIN 2G

Fried to perfection and lightly sprinkled with sea salt, this recipe is sure to become a family favorite. Serve alone or with a side of Guacamole (page 132).

1. Peel the plantains and slice into ¼-inch discs.

2. In a skillet over medium heat, heat the coconut oil.

3. Once the skillet is hot, add the sliced plantains in one layer.

4. Fry for 1 to 2 minutes per side. Using tongs or a fork, remove the fried plantains to a paper towel–lined plate to drain excess oil.

5. Sprinkle with salt and serve.

Stuffed Mushrooms

SERVES 4 TO 6 / PREP TIME: 15 MINUTES / COOK TIME: 45 MINUTES

16 white button
 mushrooms, stemmed

3 tablespoons extra-virgin
 olive oil, divided

1 pound ground sausage

¾ white onion, minced

2 garlic cloves, minced

2 teaspoons dried parsley

½ cup almond meal

Sea salt

Freshly ground
 black pepper

IN MENU FOR WEEK:

 3

PER SERVING:
CALORIES 569
TOTAL FAT 49G
SODIUM 914MG
CARBS 7G
SUGARS 3G
PROTEIN 27G

*These hors d'oeuvres will be quickly gobbled up at any party,
large or small. Packed with flavor, as well as several of the
B vitamins, they are sure to please every guest.*

1. Preheat the oven to 350°F.

2. Line a baking sheet with parchment paper.

3. In a medium bowl, combine the mushroom caps and
 2 tablespoons of olive oil.

4. In a large skillet over medium-high heat, heat the
 remaining 1 tablespoon of olive oil.

5. Cook the ground sausage in the olive oil until cooked
 through, about 7 minutes.

6. Add the onion, garlic, and parsley to the sausage
 mixture, and stir to combine.

7. Slowly add the almond meal to the pan while stirring.
 Season with salt and pepper.

8. Place the mushroom caps on the parchment paper–
 lined baking sheet, insides facing up.

9. Using a spoon, fill each cap with the stuffing mixture.
 The mixture should be overflowing the top, but
 compacted enough into the cap so that it will not fall
 out while baking.

10. Bake the mushroom caps for 30 minutes. If necessary,
 add more time to ensure the stuffing is browned. Serve.

Quick Fish Sticks

SERVES 4 / PREP TIME: 15 MINUTES / COOK TIME: 10 MINUTES

This easy recipe will transform your idea of fish sticks from a frozen, flavorless childhood snack to a sophisticated treat appropriate for eaters of any age.

1. Using paper towels, pat the cod strips until they are dry.
2. In a medium bowl, whisk the eggs.
3. Put the almond flour on a plate, and season with salt and pepper. Use a fork to combine.
4. In a large pan over medium heat, heat the coconut oil.
5. Dip each fish strip into the egg mixture, then into the almond flour mixture.
6. Place the strips on a piece of parchment paper.
7. Carefully lay the fish sticks in the pan to fry.
8. Use a thick spatula to flip the fish sticks, allowing them to brown on each side, about 3 minutes.
9. Using the spatula, remove the fish sticks from the hot oil to a paper towel–lined plate.
10. Serve immediately.

1 pound cod, deboned and cut into strips

2 eggs

1 cup almond flour

Sea salt

Freshly ground black pepper

4 tablespoons coconut oil

PER SERVING:
CALORIES 448
TOTAL FAT 32G
SODIUM 178MG
CARBS 5G
SUGARS 1G
PROTEIN 29G

Spinach Artichoke Turkey Meatballs

SERVES 4 TO 6 / PREP TIME: 20 MINUTES / COOK TIME: 20 MINUTES

1 teaspoon extra-virgin
 olive oil

1 (14-ounce) can artichoke
 hearts, chopped

½ cup fresh
 spinach, chopped

¼ teaspoon onion powder

1 pound ground turkey

1 teaspoon dried parsley

Sea salt

Freshly ground
 black pepper

PER SERVING:
CALORIES 279
TOTAL FAT 14G
SODIUM 276MG
CARBS 11G
SUGARS 1G
PROTEIN 34G

There's a restaurant near my hometown that serves an amazing turkey burger with artichokes on top. I decided to try my hand at turning that idea into a mini meatball—and they were a big hit.

1. Preheat the oven to 350°F.

2. Line a baking sheet with parchment paper.

3. In a medium pan over medium heat, sauté the olive oil, artichoke hearts, spinach, and onion powder.

4. Cook for 5 minutes, and remove the pan from the heat.

5. Let the mixture cool for 10 minutes.

6. In a large bowl, combine the ground turkey and parsley with your hands, and season with salt and pepper. Add the artichoke mixture, and mix well.

7. Form 16 equal-size meatballs, and place them on the baking sheet.

8. Bake for 20 minutes.

9. Remove from the oven, and serve immediately.

Mini Burger Sliders

SERVES 2 TO 4 / PREP TIME: 5 MINUTES / COOK TIME: 10 MINUTES

"Mini" versions always seem to be on trend, and these mini burgers are no different. They're so easy to throw together—and so yummy to eat—you won't want to share them.

1. Heat the grill or a grill pan on the stove over medium heat.
2. In a large bowl, combine the ground beef and Burger Seasoning using your hands.
3. Form burger patties 2 inches in diameter and half an inch thick.
4. Grill the patties, flipping halfway through.
5. Break the leaves of lettuce in half.
6. Place a patty on each half leaf, and top each with tomato slice.
7. Wrap the lettuce around each patty to form a sleeve.
8. Serve immediately.

1 pound ground beef

1 tablespoon Burger Seasoning (page 222)

4 leaves iceberg lettuce

1 tomato, cut into ¼-inch-thick slices

IN MENU FOR WEEK:

4

PER SERVING:
CALORIES 446
TOTAL FAT 15G
SODIUM 1090MG
CARBS 6G
SUGARS 2G
PROTEIN 70G

SIDES

Rainbow Cole Slaw

SERVES 6 / PREP TIME: 10 MINUTES

1 head purple cabbage,
    finely chopped

2½ carrots, shredded

¼ cup raisins

1 cup extra-virgin olive oil

1 tablespoon honey

¼ cup apple cider vinegar

¾ teaspoon garlic powder

¼ teaspoon onion powder

PER SERVING:
CALORIES 360
TOTAL FAT 34G
SODIUM 40MG
CARBS 18G
SUGARS 18G
PROTEIN 2G

Dairy-free and full of flavor, this vibrant side dish is as attractive as it is delicious. And of course, eating a rainbow of produce means getting a wide variety of vitamins and minerals, too.

1. Using paper towels or a colander, remove the extra water from the chopped cabbage and shredded carrots.

2. In a large bowl, stir together the cabbage, carrots, and raisins.

3. In a small bowl, whisk together the olive oil, honey, apple cider vinegar, garlic powder, and onion powder.

4. Pour the liquid mixture over the slaw mixture, toss to coat, and serve.

Baked Zucchini Fritters

SERVES 4 / PREP TIME: 15 MINUTES / COOK TIME: 15 MINUTES

Sweet and savory, these zucchini fritters are the perfect replacement for a basket of rolls at your next meal. They also make a delicious snack all on their own.

1. Preheat the oven to 400°F.

2. Using a cheese grater, shred the zucchini; then use a towel to drain the excess water.

3. In a large bowl, mix together the zucchini, egg, onion, almond flour, and Italian seasoning until well combined. Season with salt and pepper.

4. Grease a mini-muffin tin with coconut oil, and fill the muffin cups with the zucchini mixture.

5. Bake for 15 minutes, or until golden brown, and serve.

1 zucchini, grated

1 egg

¼ yellow onion

⅔ cup almond flour

1 teaspoon Italian seasoning

Sea salt

Freshly ground black pepper

Coconut oil, for greasing

Cooking Tip: *To avoid a mushy center, be sure to drain all excess water from the zucchini before combining it with the other ingredients.*

PER SERVING:
CALORIES 175
TOTAL FAT 14G
SODIUM 79MG
CARBS 6G
SUGARS 2G
PROTEIN 2G

Cauliflower Rice

SERVES 4 / PREP TIME: 10 MINUTES / COOK TIME: 15 MINUTES

1 head cauliflower

1 tablespoon coconut oil

1 garlic clove

Sea salt

**Freshly ground
  black pepper**

Cooking Tip: *For an extra kick of flavor, add ½ teaspoon onion powder, ⅓ cup cilantro, and the juice of 1 lime.*

Make-Ahead Tip: *Make a big batch of Cauliflower Rice, and freeze the extra so you'll always have some on hand. To reheat, thaw and warm on the stove with a little coconut oil.*

IN MENU FOR WEEKS:

PER SERVING:
CALORIES 47
TOTAL FAT 34G
SODIUM 79MG
CARBS 4G
SUGARS 2G
PROTEIN 1G

This recipe can easily replace starchy vegetables and grains, and it makes an excellent side dish with just about any meal. Use a bed of Cauliflower Rice under stew or chili, or as the base for a Taco and Rice Bowl (page 194).

1. Using the large holes of a cheese grater, grate the head of cauliflower.

2. In a large pan over medium heat, heat the coconut oil.

3. Add the garlic, and heat until browned.

4. Add the grated cauliflower, and cook for 9 to 12 minutes, stirring regularly.

5. Season with salt and pepper and serve.

Mashed Cauliflower

SERVES 4 / PREP TIME: 10 MINUTES / COOK TIME: 10 MINUTES

Cauliflower is one of the most versatile vegetables you can have in your fridge. Here it creates a delicious substitute for mashed white potatoes. Add roasted garlic for a little extra flavor.

1. Bring a large pot of water to a boil over high heat. Season with salt.

2. While the water is heating up, cut the cauliflower into small florets.

3. Add the cauliflower to the pot, and cook for 10 minutes. The cauliflower will be very tender.

4. Drain the florets, reserving ¼ cup of the water in a small dish.

5. In a food processor, purée the cauliflower on low, slowly streaming in the olive oil and reserved water, until smooth. Scrape down the sides of the food processor as needed to incorporate all the cauliflower.

6. Season with salt and pepper, and serve immediately.

Sea salt

1 head cauliflower

1 tablespoon extra-virgin olive oil

Freshly ground black pepper

IN MENU FOR WEEK:

3

PER SERVING:
CALORIES 47
TOTAL FAT 4G
SODIUM 78MG
CARBS 4G
SUGARS 2G
PROTEIN 1G

Tomato Basil Salad

SERVES 4 / PREP TIME: 5 MINUTES

3 cups cherry tomatoes

**3 tablespoons fresh
  basil, chopped**

**1 tablespoon extra-virgin
  olive oil**

Sea salt

IN MENU FOR WEEK:

 4

PER SERVING:
CALORIES 55
TOTAL FAT 4G
SODIUM 65MG
CARBS 5G
SUGARS 4G
PROTEIN 1G

This simple side salad is reminiscent of the classic tomato, basil, and mozzarella dish often found in Italian restaurants. Forego the cheese and let the flavors of fresh basil and tomatoes take the lead.

1. In a medium bowl, gently stir together the cherry tomatoes, basil, and olive oil until all ingredients are fully coated and combined.

2. Season with salt and serve.

Mashed Sweet Potatoes

SERVES 4 / PREP TIME: 5 MINUTES / COOK TIME: 60 MINUTES

4 sweet potatoes

**1 tablespoon
grass-fed butter**

½ teaspoon cinnamon

1 tablespoon coconut milk

Sea salt

**Freshly ground
black pepper**

IN MENU FOR WEEK:

 3

PER SERVING:
CALORIES 372
TOTAL FAT 2G
SODIUM 94MG
CARBS 84G
SUGARS 2G
PROTEIN 5G

Instead of loading my mashed sweet potatoes with maple syrup and honey, I like to keep them simple, playing off the sweet flavors naturally found in these root vegetables. These are most definitely not your grandmother's sweet potatoes.

1. Preheat the oven to 400°F.

2. Using a fork, pierce each potato several times around its surface.

3. Line a baking sheet with aluminum foil. Place the potatoes on the baking sheet, and bake for 1 hour.

4. Remove the potatoes from the oven, and allow them to cool for 5 minutes.

5. Carefully slice each potato down the middle, and remove scoop out the flesh with a spoon.

6. In a large bowl, use a potato masher to combine the potato flesh, butter, cinnamon, coconut milk, salt, and pepper, scraping down the sides of the bowl as needed to ensure you are incorporating all the sweet potatoes.

Honey-Roasted Sweet Potatoes

SERVES 4 / PREP TIME: 10 MINUTES / COOK TIME: 25 MINUTES

These roasted sweet potatoes are a favorite in our house. In fact, no matter how many extra potatoes I make, half of them seem to disappear off the tray before they make it to the table. These roasted potatoes are just as yummy served with breakfast as they are with dinner.

1. Preheat the oven to 375°F.
2. Peel the sweet potatoes, and slice them into ¼-inch-thick slices.
3. Place the cut potatoes, honey, olive oil, cinnamon, salt, and pepper in a large plastic bag.
4. Seal the bag and shake it, coating the potatoes in the seasoning.
5. Line a baking sheet with aluminum foil, and pour the potatoes onto the baking sheet.
6. Roast the potatoes for 25 minutes, flipping the slices halfway through the cooking time. Serve.

2 sweet potatoes, peeled and diced

2 tablespoons honey

2 tablespoons extra-virgin olive oil

1 teaspoon cinnamon

½ teaspoon sea salt

½ teaspoon freshly ground black pepper

IN MENU FOR WEEK:

PER SERVING:
CALORIES 271
TOTAL FAT 7G
SODIUM 248MG
CARBS 51G
SUGARS 9G
PROTEIN 2G

Spicy and Sweet Fries

SERVES 4 / PREP TIME: 10 MINUTES / COOK TIME: 30 MINUTES

I like crispy fries that are perfectly crunchy on the outside and tender on the inside. Unfortunately, most homemade sweet potato fries go limp. The wire rack technique I explain below will help you achieve an evenly baked, crispy batch of fries every time.

1. Preheat the oven to 425°F.
2. Peel the sweet potatoes, and cut them into thin wedges.
3. In a large bowl, use tongs or two forks to toss the potatoes together with the olive oil, salt, cumin, chili powder, and cayenne pepper, coating the potatoes thoroughly in the seasoning mixture.
4. Line a baking sheet with parchment paper, and place a wire rack on top so the surface is elevated off the baking sheet.
5. Place the potato wedges on the wire rack.
6. Bake for 30 minutes, flipping the wedges halfway through the cooking time.

2 pounds sweet potatoes

3 tablespoons extra-virgin olive oil

1½ teaspoons sea salt

¼ teaspoon cumin

¼ teaspoon chili powder

Dash cayenne pepper

Cooking Tip: *If your fries are still a bit soft after baking, next time try soaking them in a bowl of ice water for 1 hour after step 2. Drain them, dry well, and then follow the instructions from step 3.*

IN MENU FOR WEEK:

 1

PER SERVING:
CALORIES 359
TOTAL FAT 11G
SODIUM 724MG
CARBS 63G
SUGARS 1G
PROTEIN 4G

Family-Style Carrots

SERVES 4 / PREP TIME: 10 MINUTES / COOK TIME: 25 MINUTES

12 carrots, peeled and chopped

4 tablespoons extra-virgin olive oil, divided

⅓ cup honey

Sea salt

Freshly ground black pepper

IN MENU FOR WEEK:

PER SERVING:
CALORIES 291
TOTAL FAT 14G
SODIUM 186MG
CARBS 44G
SUGARS 35G
PROTEIN 2G

Roasted in honey until perfectly crisp, these carrots are aptly named, as they will be loved by the whole family. Gone are the days of hiding vegetables in napkins and feeding them to the dog.

1. Preheat the oven to 450°F.

2. Using 1 tablespoon of olive oil, coat a baking sheet. Place the carrots in a single layer on the sheet.

3. In a small bowl, whisk together the remaining 3 table-spoons of olive oil and the honey, and season with salt and pepper.

4. Pour the oil mixture over the carrots, coating them evenly.

5. Bake the carrots for 10 minutes.

6. Remove the baking sheet from the oven, and carefully stir the carrots.

7. Place the sheet back in the oven, bake for an additional 15 minutes, and serve.

Roasted Broccoli

SERVES 4 / PREP TIME: 10 MINUTES / COOK TIME: 20 MINUTES

I used to avoid vegetables at all cost—until I learned how to roast them properly. This roasting technique also works with asparagus, cauliflower, and an endless variety of other vegetables. Pick your favorite, or simply use what you have in the fridge.

1. Preheat the oven to 425°F.

2. Line a baking sheet with parchment paper.

3. Cut the broccoli into florets or small bunches.

4. In a large bowl, toss together the broccoli, garlic, olive oil, and lemon juice, and season with salt and pepper.

5. Spread the broccoli in a single layer on the baking sheet and roast for 20 minutes.

6. Remove the baking sheet from the oven, and season with some additional pepper before serving.

1 head broccoli

3 garlic cloves, minced

4 tablespoons extra-virgin olive oil

Juice of ½ lemon

Sea salt

Freshly ground black pepper

IN MENU FOR WEEKS:

PER SERVING:
CALORIES 170
TOTAL FAT 15G
SODIUM 104MG
CARBS 10G
SUGARS 2G
PROTEIN 4G

Bacon-Wrapped Asparagus

SERVES 4 / PREP TIME: 10 MINUTES / COOK TIME: 12 MINUTES

1½ pounds asparagus

1 tablespoon extra-virgin olive oil

Freshly ground black pepper

4 strips bacon

PER SERVING:
CALORIES 167
TOTAL FAT 12G
SODIUM 442MG
CARBS 7G
SUGARS 3G
PROTEIN 11G

I am a firm believer that everything tastes better with bacon—fruit, vegetables, and baked goods included. This recipe is no exception, pairing crispy bacon with fresh roasted asparagus.

1. Preheat the oven to 400°F.

2. Line a baking sheet with edges with parchment paper, and place a wire rack on top so the surface is elevated off the baking sheet.

3. Trim the asparagus by holding the stalks at each end and snapping. Discard the ends of the stems. You will want to have a number of stalks that is divisible by 4.

4. Place the asparagus tips in a large plastic bag with the olive oil and season with pepper. Toss to combine the ingredients and coat the asparagus.

5. Wrap 1 strip of bacon around a bundle of asparagus, spreading the bacon so there is only 1 layer of bacon at any point on the bundle.

6. Repeat with the 3 remaining bundles.

7. Place the bundles on the wire rack, bake for 12 minutes, and serve.

Sautéed Spinach and Mushrooms

SERVES 4 / PREP TIME: 5 MINUTES / COOK TIME: 15 MINUTES

If you're looking for an especially quick side dish that works with a variety of flavors, this one's for you! The soft spinach matches perfectly with the snappy bite of the baby mushrooms.

1. In a large pan over medium heat, heat 2 tablespoons of olive oil.

2. Add the mushrooms, and cook for 7 minutes, stirring occasionally.

3. Add the remaining tablespoon of olive oil and the garlic and shallot, and stir to combine.

4. Cook for an additional 4 minutes.

5. Add the spinach, and stir to combine.

6. Sauté the spinach for 2 minutes, until it is wilted.

7. Season with salt and pepper before serving.

3 tablespoons extra-virgin olive oil, divided

½ pound baby mushrooms

2 garlic cloves, minced

1 shallot, minced

1 (10-ounce) package baby spinach

Sea salt

Freshly ground black pepper

IN MENU FOR WEEK:

 4

PER SERVING:
CALORIES 122
TOTAL FAT 11G
SODIUM 118MG
CARBS 5G
SUGARS 1G
PROTEIN 4G

Roasted Brussels Sprouts with Bacon

SERVES 4 / PREP TIME: 10 MINUTES / COOK TIME: 35 MINUTES

1 pound Brussels sprouts, trimmed and halved lengthwise

2 tablespoons extra-virgin olive oil

½ teaspoon sea salt

⅓ teaspoon freshly ground black pepper

6 bacon strips, chopped

Cooking Tip: *For a little added flair whip up a batch of Garlic Aioli (page 224) and serve on the side.*

IN MENU FOR WEEK:

 2

PER SERVING:
CALORIES 263
TOTAL FAT 19G
SODIUM 921MG
CARBS 11G
SUGARS 3G
PROTEIN 14G

A little tapas place near our house serves the most decadent roasted Brussels sprouts I have ever tasted. This recipe tastes just as indulgent, and you can enjoy it without the guilt.

1. Preheat the oven to 400°F.

2. Line a baking sheet with parchment paper.

3. In a large bowl, toss together the Brussels sprouts, olive oil, salt, and pepper.

4. Spread the Brussels sprouts in a single layer on the baking sheet.

5. Sprinkle the chopped bacon on top of the Brussels sprouts and roast for 35 minutes.

6. Remove the Brussels sprouts from the oven, and serve immediately.

Lemon Zest Grilled Squash

SERVES 8 / PREP TIME: 15 MINUTES / COOK TIME: 20 MINUTES

6 yellow squash

¼ cup extra-virgin olive oil

2 teaspoons sea salt, divided

1 teaspoon freshly ground black pepper

Juice and zest of 2 lemons

IN MENU FOR WEEKS:

PER SERVING:
CALORIES 78
TOTAL FAT 7G
SODIUM 483MG
CARBS 5G
SUGARS 3G
PROTEIN 2G

Lightly seasoned with lemon zest and salt, this simple vegetable dish features the fresh summer squash as its main event. This brightly flavored side dish pairs well with barbecued meats and seafood alike.

1. Slice the ends off of each squash, and cut lengthwise into ¼-inch-thick slices.

2. In a large plastic bag, combine the squash, olive oil, 1 teaspoon of salt, pepper, and the lemon juice, and toss to coat.

3. Prepare the grill or grill pan to medium-low heat, and grill the squash on both sides until tender.

4. Once the squash is cooked (be careful not to burn), place the slices on a plate, and sprinkle with the lemon zest and the remaining teaspoon of salt. Serve.

Roasted Acorn Squash

SERVES 4 / PREP TIME: 5 MINUTES / COOK TIME: 1 HOUR

Something about roasted squash just screams "winter." But what's great about acorn squash is that you can find it at stores year round. This is a quick and easy recipe that both beginners and squash aficionados will love.

1. Preheat the oven to 350°F.
2. Line a baking sheet with aluminum foil.
3. Using a large, sharp knife, cut the squash in half.
4. Using a large spoon, scoop out the seeds from each of the halves.
5. Using your hands, rub both the inside and outside surfaces of the halves with the coconut oil.
6. Place the squash cut-side down on the baking sheet, and bake for 60 minutes.
7. Remove the squash halves from the oven. Using a butter knife, slice cross sections into the flesh of the squash.
8. Scoop out the squash cubes, and serve sprinkled with cinnamon and nutmeg.

1 acorn squash

1 teaspoon coconut oil

Cinnamon, for sprinkling

Nutmeg, for sprinkling

IN MENU FOR WEEK:

2

PER SERVING:
CALORIES 53
TOTAL FAT 1G
SODIUM 3MG
CARBS 11G
SUGARS 0G
PROTEIN 1G

ENTRÉES

Zucchini and Spaghetti Squash Medley

SERVES 3 / PREP TIME: 20 MINUTES / COOK TIME: 40 MINUTES

1 spaghetti squash

2 tablespoons extra-virgin
  olive oil

1 zucchini

3 garlic cloves, minced

Sea salt

Freshly ground
  black pepper

⅓ cup pine nuts,
  toasted (optional)

Cooking Tip: *Pick up an inexpensive julienne peeler or vegetable spiralizer, or, to make this recipe without one of these tools, simply slice the zucchini very thinly using a knife—just be extra careful.*

PER SERVING:
CALORIES 253
TOTAL FAT 22G
SODIUM 108MG
CARBS 15G
SUGARS 2G
PROTEIN 4G

Squash is the main event in this dish. It's not too heavy, and it's perfect for the summer when squash is abundant and at the peak of its harvest season. If you don't already have a julienne peeler for creating vegetable noodles, pick one up—I promise your life will never be the same.

1. Preheat the oven to 425°F.

2. Cut the spaghetti squash in half lengthwise.

3. Using a large spoon, scrape out all the seeds and loose fibers from each half.

4. Line a baking sheet with aluminum foil.

5. Place the spaghetti squash face down on the baking sheet, and bake for 35 minutes.

6. Remove the squash from the oven, and turn the halves over so they are face up. Allow them to cool for 5 minutes.

7. Scrape the insides of the squash halves with a large fork to create "spaghetti."

8. In a large pan over medium heat, heat the olive oil.

9. Using a vegetable spiralizer or julienne peeler, create thin noodles from the zucchini.

10. Place the julienned zucchini and the garlic in the pan, and cook uncovered for 90 seconds.

11. Season with salt and pepper, and cover the pan. Cook for 3 minutes, until the zucchini is soft.

12. Scoop the "spaghetti" strands into the pan, and stir. Turn the heat to low, and cook for another minute.

13. Remove the pan from the heat, top with the toasted pine nuts (if using), and serve.

Shrimp Scampi over Zucchini Noodles

SERVES 4 / PREP TIME: 15 MINUTES / COOK TIME: 20 MINUTES

Zucchini noodles are a great alternative to traditional pasta and are simple to make. Other possible replacements include carrot noodles (prepared the same way as the zucchini is) or spaghetti squash.

1. Using a vegetable spiralizer or julienne peeler, create thin noodles from the zucchini.

2. In a large pan over medium heat, melt the butter.

3. Add the garlic, and sauté until the garlic is lightly browned.

4. Turn the heat up to high, and add the zucchini and shrimp.

5. Using metal tongs, toss the zucchini and shrimp until the shrimp are fully cooked.

6. Season with pepper.

7. Remove the pan from the heat, and serve immediately.

4 zucchini

¼ cup grass-fed butter

10 garlic cloves, minced

1 pound raw shrimp, peeled and deveined

Freshly ground black pepper

Cooking Tip: *The zucchini will release some water while cooking, making additional sauce. For a richer sauce, add more butter. Do so slowly and in 1-tablespoon increments as you cook, so you can achieve your perfect consistency.*

IN MENU FOR WEEK:

 1

PER SERVING:
CALORIES 213
TOTAL FAT 6G
SODIUM 330MG
CARBS 12G
SUGARS 4G
PROTEIN 30G

Coconut Shrimp

SERVES 4 / PREP TIME: 15 MINUTES / COOK TIME: 10 MINUTES

¼ cup arrowroot powder

2 large eggs

¾ cup almond flour

1 cup unsweetened
  shredded coconut

Sea salt

Freshly ground
  black pepper

1 pound large raw shrimp,
  peeled and deveined

3 tablespoons coconut oil

IN MENU FOR WEEK:

 2

PER SERVING:
CALORIES 565
TOTAL FAT 40G
SODIUM 245MG
CARBS 20G
SUGARS 3G
PROTEIN 26G

Crisp on the outside and bursting with flavor within, this recipe offers a surefire technique for preparing mouthwatering shrimp. Enjoy them on their own, pile them on top of zucchini noodles, or stuff them into a lettuce wrap. They are a crowd pleaser no matter how you serve them.

1. Pour the arrowroot powder onto a medium plate.

2. In a medium bowl, whisk the eggs.

3. On a medium plate, combine the almond flour and shredded coconut, and season with salt and pepper.

4. Dip each shrimp into the arrowroot powder, then the egg, and then into the almond flour and coconut mixture.

5. In a large skillet over medium heat, heat the coconut oil.

6. Place the shrimp in the hot coconut oil, and cook for 2 minutes on one side.

7. Flip the shrimp, and cook for an additional 2 minutes.

8. When the shrimp have finished cooking, remove them from the oil, drain on a paper towel–lined plate, and serve.

Simple Scallops

SERVES 6 / PREP TIME: 5 MINUTES / COOK TIME: 10 MINUTES

I used to think preparing seafood was a tedious task, but this extra-simple recipe can be on the table in 15 minutes or less. Pair with a simple side salad for a light and refreshing meal.

1. In a medium pan over medium heat, melt the butter.

2. Add the garlic, and sauté until fragrant, about 1 minute.

3. Carefully place the scallops in the butter. Cook for 4 minutes on each side—the scallops will be opaque white.

4. Remove the scallops from the pan to a plate.

5. In the same pan, add the lemon juice and season with salt and pepper.

6. Pour the lemon sauce over the scallops and serve.

¾ cup grass-fed butter

15 garlic cloves, minced

2 pounds scallops

2 tablespoons freshly squeezed lemon juice

Sea salt

Freshly ground black pepper

IN MENU FOR WEEK:

 4

PER SERVING:
CALORIES 217
TOTAL FAT 9G
SODIUM 349MG
CARBS 8G
SUGARS 2G
PROTEIN 28G

Sweet Potato Gnocchi

SERVES 4 / PREP TIME: 45 MINUTES / COOK TIME: 10 MINUTES

2 sweet potatoes

1¾ cups almond flour

1 cup arrowroot powder, divided

1 teaspoon sea salt

1 teaspoon baking soda

Pinch garlic powder

1 egg white

IN MENU FOR WEEK:

 3

PER SERVING:
CALORIES 637
TOTAL FAT 27G
SODIUM 804MG
CARBS 83G
SUGARS 3G
PROTEIN 3G

Gnocchi has always been my pasta of choice, so I created this version as an alternative to the traditional white potato and flour. Using sweet potatoes as a base in this recipe provides so much flavor. All you need to add is a little butter instead of a pile of sauce.

1. Preheat the oven to 400°F.
2. Pierce each sweet potato multiple times with a fork. Place them on a cookie sheet, and bake for 35 minutes.
3. Bring a large pot of water to a boil.
4. Use a spoon to scoop the flesh out of the potatoes and into a medium bowl. Discard the skins.
5. Mash the potatoes until there are no lumps.
6. Add the almond flour, ¾ cup of arrowroot powder, salt, baking soda, and garlic powder to the mashed sweet potatoes. Mix well to combine.
7. Gently mix the egg white into the mixture until a ball of dough is formed.
8. Spread the remaining ¼ cup of arrowroot powder onto a piece of wax paper.
9. Divide the dough into 2 equal parts.
10. Place 1 piece of the dough on the wax paper, and roll it within the paper to create a cylinder.
11. Unwrap the gnocchi dough from the wax paper, and use a knife to cut it into ½-inch-wide pieces.
12. Repeat steps 10 and 11 with the second piece of dough.
13. Place the gnocchi slices in the boiling water, and cook for 2 minutes.
14. Using a slotted spoon, remove the gnocchi from the water and serve immediately.

Lemon Butter Cod

SERVES 4 / PREP TIME: 5 MINUTES / COOK TIME: 10 MINUTES

4 tablespoons grass-fed butter, divided

1 garlic clove, minced

1 pound cod

1 teaspoon dried parsley

Sea salt

Freshly ground black pepper

Juice of 1 lemon

1 cup chicken stock

1 lemon, cut into ¼-inch-thick slices

IN MENU FOR WEEK:

PER SERVING:
CALORIES 163
TOTAL FAT 5G
SODIUM 370MG
CARBS 3G
SUGARS 2G
PROTEIN 27G

A simple lemon butter cod is the perfect dish when you're looking to switch things up in the protein department. Lightly seasoned and sautéed, this is a savory dish that takes no time at all.

1. In a large pan over low heat, melt 2 tablespoons of butter.

2. Add the garlic to the pan, and sauté for 30 seconds.

3. Season the cod with the parsley, salt, and pepper.

4. Turn the heat up to medium-high, and add the cod. Sauté on each side for 2 minutes.

5. Remove the cod from the pan, and plate the pieces.

6. Pour the lemon juice and chicken stock into the pan, and bring the liquid to a boil.

7. Add the remaining 2 tablespoons of butter, and whisk until the sauce is well blended.

8. Once the butter is melted, add the lemon slices and sauté for 45 seconds.

9. Add 1 slice of lemon onto each slice of cod, pour the sauce over the plates, and serve.

Chicken Fried Rice

SERVES 4 / PREP TIME: 5 MINUTES / COOK TIME: 11 MINUTES

This remake of the takeout classic is everything you're looking for in a quick and easy weeknight meal. Add in fresh broccoli, carrots, and any other vegetables you have on hand.

1. In a large mixing bowl, stir together the Cauliflower Rice, egg, coconut flour, salt, and pepper.

2. In a large saucepan, heat the coconut oil over medium-high heat.

3. Carefully place the diced chicken in the hot oil, and stir to ensure each piece is fully cooked.

4. Once the chicken is cooked, add the red onion, garlic powder, and basil. Cook for 30 seconds.

5. Add the Cauliflower Rice mixture to the same saucepan, and stir to combine all ingredients.

6. Sauté for 10 minutes and serve.

3 cups Cauliflower Rice (page 150)

1 egg

2 tablespoons coconut flour

1 teaspoon sea salt

½ teaspoon freshly ground black pepper

3 tablespoons coconut oil

1 pound boneless chicken breasts, diced

½ red onion, minced

1½ teaspoons garlic powder

2 teaspoons dried basil

PER SERVING:
CALORIES 393
TOTAL FAT 24G
SODIUM 668MG
CARBS 8G
SUGARS 3G
PROTEIN 37G

Easy Roasted Chicken

SERVES 8 / PREP TIME: 10 MINUTES / COOK TIME: 1 HOUR 15 MINUTES

1 (5-pound) whole chicken, neck and giblets removed

1½ tablespoons extra-virgin olive oil

3 garlic cloves, chopped

1 teaspoon dried thyme

Sea salt

Freshly ground black pepper

1 lemon, cut into ¼-inch-thick slices

IN MENU FOR WEEK:

PER SERVING:
CALORIES 563
TOTAL FAT 24G
SODIUM 275MG
CARBS 1G
SUGARS 0G
PROTEIN 82G

Roasting a whole bird is a skill that every kitchen cook should master. This recipe is simple yet always a winner. Impress at your next family gathering; then use the leftover meat for soups and lettuce wraps.

1. Preheat the oven to 425°F, with the rack in the middle.
2. Place the whole chicken on a cutting board.
3. Using paper towels, dry off the whole chicken.
4. Drizzle the olive oil onto the skin of the chicken, and use your hands to coat the entire bird.
5. In a small bowl, combine the garlic and thyme, and season with salt and pepper.
6. Place the garlic spice mixture and the lemon slices inside the cavity.
7. Season the outside of the chicken with additional salt and pepper.
8. Place the chicken in a roasting pan with the breast-side facing up.
9. Roast in the oven for 15 minutes. Reduce the heat to 350°F, and roast for an additional 60 minutes.
10. Use a meat thermometer in the thigh to check the temperature. The chicken is ready to take out when the thermometer reads 165°F.
11. Remove the chicken from the oven, and allow it to rest for 10 minutes before carving and serving.

Slow Cooker Salsa Chicken

SERVES 4 / PREP TIME: 5 MINUTES / COOK TIME: 4 TO 7 HOURS

This recipe is so simple, I almost feel guilty calling it a recipe at all. We make this dish at least once a week when we just need something quick with minimal effort. Serve it over a bed of Cauliflower Rice (page 150) or in a lettuce wrap with sliced avocado.

1. Place the chicken in the bottom of a slow cooker.
2. In a small bowl, stir together the cumin, chili powder, and cayenne pepper along with salt and pepper.
3. Pour the seasoning mixture over the chicken.
4. Add the Salsa to the bottom of the slow cooker.
5. Cook on high for 4 hours or low for 7 hours.
6. When you are ready to eat, shred the chicken with two forks. Stir to coat the chicken with the Salsa and serve.

2 pounds boneless chicken breasts

1½ tablespoons cumin

1½ tablespoons chili powder

¼ teaspoon cayenne pepper

Sea salt

Freshly ground black pepper

2 cups Salsa (page 236)

Cooking Tip: *Save some time by making the Salsa in advance or using a fresh store-bought version.*

IN MENU FOR WEEK:

2

PER SERVING:
CALORIES 484
TOTAL FAT 18G
SODIUM 1066MG
CARBS 11G
SUGARS 4G
PROTEIN 68G

Spicy Grilled Shrimp Kebabs

SERVES 6 / PREP TIME: 10 MINUTES / COOK TIME: 5 MINUTES

Kebabs make for a speedy dish that is not only a snap to assemble but also fun to eat. They are a great option to cook for a party because the food is pre-portioned and can be eaten with your hands. Serve with Chimichurri and enjoy!

1. Preheat the grill or a grill pan to medium-high heat.
2. Thread each shrimp onto a wooden skewer. Place the skewers in a dish with sides.
3. In a small bowl, whisk together the olive oil, garlic, crushed red pepper flakes, onion powder, salt, pepper, and lemon juice.
4. Pour the marinade over the skewers.
5. Grill the skewers for 2 minutes on one side, then turn over and repeat. Serve.

12 jumbo raw shrimp, peeled and deveined

2 tablespoons extra-virgin olive oil

5 garlic cloves, minced

¼ teaspoon crushed red pepper flakes

1 teaspoon onion powder

1 teaspoon sea salt

1 teaspoon freshly ground black pepper

Juice of 1 lemon

Cooking Tip: *If you don't eat shrimp, you can easily replace the shrimp with chicken or beef. Veggie-only kebabs also make a great side dish.*

IN MENU FOR WEEK:

 2

PER SERVING:
CALORIES 72
TOTAL FAT 5G
SODIUM 257MG
CARBS 1G
SUGARS 0G
PROTEIN 7G

Mexican Chicken Burgers

SERVES 6 / PREP TIME: 5 MINUTES / COOK TIME: 15 MINUTES

2 pounds ground chicken

4 tablespoons Taco Seasoning (page 221)

½ white onion, diced

1 teaspoon minced garlic cloves

2 eggs

Sea salt

Freshly ground black pepper

Guacamole (page 132), for garnish

This recipe is a fiesta in a burger. All the flavors of your favorite Mexican dish combine in a burger that's quick to make and easy to enjoy.

1. In a large bowl, combine the chicken, Taco Seasoning, onion, garlic cloves, and eggs, and season with salt and pepper. Stir well to incorporate the egg completely.

2. Heat the grill or a grill pan to medium heat.

3. Using your hands, form the meat mixture into 6 patties.

4. Grill on each side until fully cooked.

5. Garnish the burgers with the Guacamole and serve.

IN MENU FOR WEEK:

 4

PER SERVING (WITHOUT GUACAMOLE): CALORIES 495
TOTAL FAT 20G
SODIUM 783MG
CARBS 6G
SUGARS 2G
PROTEIN 70G

Crispy Chicken Tenders

SERVES 4 / PREP TIME: 5 MINUTES / COOK TIME: 18 MINUTES

This is one recipe no Paleo cook should be without. Crispy on the outside and tender on the inside, these chicken tenders were created with the little Paleo eaters in mind. You can whip up a batch of these healthy chicken tenders in less time than it takes to cook the prepackaged version.

1. Preheat the oven to 425°F.
2. Line a baking sheet with parchment paper, and place a wire rack on top.
3. In a small bowl, whisk the eggs.
4. In a shallow dish, use a fork to mix the almond meal, salt, garlic powder, and onion powder.
5. Dip the chicken into the egg, then into the almond meal mixture, and place it on the wire rack. Repeat with each piece.
6. Bake for 18 minutes and serve.

2 eggs

1 cup almond flour

1 teaspoon sea salt

1 teaspoon garlic powder

1 teaspoon onion powder

2 pounds chicken tenders

Make-Ahead Tip: *Double the recipe, and keep the leftovers in an airtight container in the fridge or freezer. These are perfect for a quick salad topping throughout the week or an easy reheat for the babysitter.*

IN MENU FOR WEEK:

 1

PER SERVING:
CALORIES 516
TOTAL FAT 21G
SODIUM 642MG
CARBS 6G
SUGARS 2G
PROTEIN 74G

Honey-Roasted Salmon

SERVES 4 / PREP TIME: 15 MINUTES / COOK TIME: 10 MINUTES

1 tablespoon honey

**2 teaspoons
coconut aminos**

1 teaspoon coconut oil

**¼ teaspoon freshly ground
black pepper**

4 wild salmon fillets

¼ cup scallions (optional)

IN MENU FOR WEEK:

 4

PER SERVING:
CALORIES 319
TOTAL FAT 16G
SODIUM 137MG
CARBS 5G
SUGARS 5G
PROTEIN 36G

Here salmon fillets are drizzled in honey and roasted for a light but decadent dish. For an easy meal, serve with a simple green salad of your favorite roasted vegetables.

1. Remove the salmon fillets from the refrigerator and allow them to come to room temperature for 10 minutes on a large plate.

2. In a small bowl, whisk together the honey, coconut aminos, coconut oil, and pepper.

3. Heat a skillet over medium-high heat.

4. Using a spoon, drizzle the honey mixture over the salmon, ensuring that it coats each piece evenly.

5. Place the salmon skin side down and cook for 5 minutes.

6. Using a spatula, turn the salmon over and cook for an additional 3 minutes.

7. Garnish with scallions and serve.

Chicken Fajitas

SERVES 4 / PREP TIME: 5 MINUTES / COOK TIME: 10 MINUTES

**1 pound boneless
chicken breast**

1 tablespoon coconut oil

**3 bell peppers, cored,
seeded, and thinly sliced**

1 onion, thinly sliced

1 teaspoon paprika

½ teaspoon chili powder

¼ teaspoon cumin

Sea salt

**Freshly ground
black pepper**

**1 head iceberg
lettuce, cored**

IN MENU FOR WEEK:

PER SERVING:
CALORIES 268
TOTAL FAT 8G
SODIUM 202MG
CARBS 11G
SUGARS 6G
PROTEIN 38G

Fajitas are always a fun dish for the whole family. Serve them up in one big bowl, or separate out the meat and veggies so everyone can get involved and wrap up their own.

1. Using a sharp knife, cut the chicken into 1-inch pieces.

2. In a large pan over medium heat, heat the coconut oil.

3. When the oil is hot, add the chicken, peppers, and onion. Sauté for 30 seconds.

4. Add the paprika, chili powder, and cumin to the pan, and season with salt and pepper. Stir to combine all of the ingredients.

5. Sauté the mixture until the chicken is fully cooked through, stirring regularly.

6. While the chicken and vegetables are cooking, separate full leaves from the head of iceberg lettuce, and place them on a plate.

7. Remove the chicken and vegetables from the stove, and put them in a medium bowl.

8. Use the lettuce leaves to create wraps for the fajita mixture and serve.

Chicken and Broccoli Stir-Fry

SERVES 4 / PREP TIME: 5 MINUTES / COOK TIME: 10 MINUTES

A play on the traditional Chinese dish, this simple stir-fry uses chicken instead of beef but delivers the same flavors. This dish is delicious on its own or served over a bed of Cauliflower Rice (page 150).

1 tablespoon sesame oil

1 tablespoon minced garlic

1 tablespoon minced ginger

1 pound boneless chicken breast, diced

¼ cup coconut aminos

1 head broccoli

1. In a large saucepan over medium-high heat, heat the sesame oil.

2. Once the oil is hot, add the garlic and ginger.

3. Sauté for 30 seconds.

4. Add the diced chicken breast and coconut aminos, and cook until browned.

5. Slice the broccoli into small florets and stem pieces.

6. Add the broccoli to the pan with the chicken, cook until tender, and serve.

IN MENU FOR WEEK:

4

PER SERVING:
CALORIES 255
TOTAL FAT 8G
SODIUM 169MG
CARBS 8G
SUGARS 2G
PROTEIN 39G

Open-Faced Portobello Turkey Burger

SERVES 4 / PREP TIME: 10 MINUTES / COOK TIME: 26 MINUTES

4 large portobello
  mushrooms

1 tablespoon coconut oil

2 pounds ground turkey

1 teaspoon cumin

1 teaspoon onion powder

1 teaspoon garlic powder

Lettuce, for garnish

Tomato, for garnish

PER SERVING:
CALORIES 499
TOTAL FAT 28G
SODIUM 244MG
CARBS 4G
SUGARS 0G
PROTEIN 65G

Burgers are a favorite in our house. They are easy to pull together and quick to cook, making them a convenient weeknight meal, but sometimes we get tired of ground beef. This version is made with ground turkey, which pairs well with a portobello mushroom bun. We like them open-faced, but add another on top, and enjoy eating with your hands.

1. Preheat the oven to 425°F.

2. Wet a paper towel, and wipe the outside of the mushrooms until they are clean.

3. Remove the stems with your hands and discard.

4. Using a spoon, scrape out the inside gills and discard them as well.

5. Brush the mushroom caps with coconut oil, and place on a foil-lined baking sheet.

6. Roast for 10 minutes with the insides facing up.

7. Flip the caps, and roast for an additional 10 minutes. Remove from the oven to cool slightly.

8. Heat the grill or a stovetop grill pan to medium.

9. In a large bowl, use your hands to combine the ground turkey, cumin, onion powder, and garlic powder.

10. Form the turkey mixture into 4 patties.

11. Grill each patty for 3 minutes on each side.

12. Place the turkey burger on top of the mushroom—inside facing up. Top the burger with lettuce and tomato and serve.

Rosemary Pork Loin

SERVES 4 / PREP TIME: 5 MINUTES / COOK TIME: 60 MINUTES

This pork loin is an excellent dish to serve when you want to impress visitors. It tastes and looks fancy—but the truth is it only takes a few minutes to prep, and the oven does the rest of the work.

1. Preheat the oven to 400°F.

2. In a small bowl, stir together the garlic, rosemary, salt, and pepper.

3. Coat the pork in its entirety with the seasoning mix.

4. Place the pork roast fat-side down in a roasting pan or baking dish lined with foil.

5. Roast the pork for 30 minutes; then turn it over.

6. Continue cooking for 25 minutes until the meat reaches 155°F.

7. Remove the pork from the oven, and let it sit for 10 minutes.

8. Cut the pork crosswise into ¼-inch-thick slices and serve.

5 garlic cloves, minced

2½ teaspoons dried rosemary

1½ teaspoons sea salt

½ teaspoon freshly ground black pepper

3 pounds boneless pork loin roast

PER SERVING:
CALORIES 495
TOTAL FAT 12G
SODIUM 897MG
CARBS 2G
SUGARS 0G
PROTEIN 89G

Fresh Rosemary Turkey

SERVES 6 / PREP TIME: 20 MINUTES / COOK TIME: 1 HOUR

Too often, turkey is reserved as a holiday bird, but with this easy-to-follow recipe, it can be enjoyed all year long. The rosemary not only lends its flavor to the delicious meat, but the aroma while it bakes will leave your house smelling divine.

1. Preheat the oven to 450°F with the rack toward the bottom.
2. Remove the turkey breast from the refrigerator, and allow it to sit at room temperature for 10 minutes.
3. Dry the turkey breast with paper towels.
4. Drizzle the olive oil onto the turkey, using your hands to coat it completely.
5. Sprinkle the rosemary, salt, and pepper onto the turkey, using your hands to rub the seasoning into the meat.
6. Place the turkey onto a rack within a foil-lined baking pan so that it is elevated off the base of the pan.
7. When the oven has preheated, turn the temperature down to 350°F; then put the turkey inside.
8. Roast for 1 hour.
9. Use a meat thermometer in the thickest part of the turkey to check the temperature. The turkey is ready to take out when the thermometer reads 165°F.
10. Remove the turkey from the oven, and allow it to sit for 15 minutes before slicing and serving.

3 pounds boneless turkey breast

2 tablespoons extra-virgin olive oil

2 tablespoons fresh rosemary, chopped

1 teaspoon sea salt

1 teaspoon freshly ground black pepper

IN MENU FOR WEEK:

 4

PER SERVING.
CALORIES 280
TOTAL FAT 9G
SODIUM 2615MG
CARBS 11G
SUGARS 8G
PROTEIN 39G

Pineapple Pulled Pork

SERVES 6 / PREP TIME: 5 MINUTES / COOK TIME: 4 TO 7 HOURS

2 pounds boneless
  pork shoulder

4 garlic cloves, peeled

¼ cup chicken broth

Juice of 2 lemons, plus zest
  of 1 lemon

1 teaspoon onion powder

½ teaspoon cayenne pepper

2 cups pineapple, diced

IN MENU FOR WEEK:

PER SERVING:
CALORIES 250
TOTAL FAT 6G
SODIUM 119MG
CARBS 8G
SUGARS 6G
PROTEIN 40G

The slow cooker is every wannabe chef's best friend, and I am not ashamed to admit I let ours do the cooking most nights of the week. After hours in the slow cooker, this pulled pork is, so tender it's falling apart and ready to melt in your mouth.

1. Place the pork, garlic cloves, chicken broth, lemon juice, lemon zest, onion powder, and cayenne pepper in a slow cooker.

2. Layer the diced pineapple on top of the pork.

3. Cook on high for 4 hours, or low for 7 hours.

4. When you are ready to eat, shred the pork with two forks. Stir to coat the pork with the sauce produced during cooking and serve.

Pork Chops

SERVES 4 / PREP TIME: 35 MINUTES / COOK TIME: 60 MINUTES

Like roasting a chicken, making pork chops is a skill I firmly believe a chef at any level should be able to master. This recipe is perfect for beginners but still packs a punch of flavor.

1. Allow the pork chops to come to room temperature on the counter for 30 minutes.
2. In a large pan over high heat, heat the olive oil.
3. Generously season both sides of the pork chops with salt and pepper.
4. Sear the pork chops for 1 minute on each side.
5. Turn the heat down to low, and add the chicken broth, onion, and garlic.
6. Cover the pan, and simmer for 1 hour.

4 pork chops

1 tablespoon extra-virgin olive oil

Sea salt

Freshly ground black pepper

1½ cups chicken broth

1 yellow onion, chopped

3 garlic cloves, chopped

IN MENU FOR WEEK:

3

PER SERVING:
CALORIES 315
TOTAL FAT 24G
SODIUM 402MG
CARBS 4G
SUGARS 1G
PROTEIN 20G

Fall-Apart Short Ribs

SERVES 6 / PREP TIME: 5 MINUTES / COOK TIME: 5 TO 8 HOURS

1 tablespoon coconut oil

¼ teaspoon garlic powder

¼ teaspoon onion powder

¼ teaspoon dried rosemary

Sea salt

Freshly ground
 black pepper

2 pounds short ribs

½ cup red wine

½ cup water

IN MENU FOR WEEK:

PER SERVING:
CALORIES 626
TOTAL FAT 57G
SODIUM 114MG
CARBS 1G
SUGARS 0G
PROTEIN 22G

Short ribs used to be my go-to on restaurant menus because I was intimidated to cook them myself. However, with this set-it-and-forget recipe, you can conquer the short rib and achieve that same restaurant taste at home.

1. In a large pan over medium-high heat, heat the coconut oil.

2. In a small bowl, mix together the garlic powder, onion powder, rosemary, salt, and pepper.

3. Dry the short ribs off, and coat them with the seasoning mixture.

4. Once the oil is extremely hot, place the short ribs in the pan.

5. Sear on all sides until they are lightly browned—for 2 minutes total.

6. Place the short ribs in a slow cooker.

7. Add the wine and water to surround the short ribs.

8. Cook on high for 5 hours, or low for 8 hours.

9. When you are ready to eat, shred the short ribs with two forks. Stir to coat the meat with the sauce produced during cooking and serve.

Stuffed Italian Burgers with Roasted Peppers and Eggplant

SERVES 4 / PREP TIME: 10 MINUTES / COOK TIME: 10 MINUTES

Many people get bored with burgers because they're afraid to experiment, but few will shy away from this tantalizing version. Full of bright and tender vegetables, this Italian-inspired burger is juicy, flavorful, and sure to please.

TO MAKE THE STUFFING

In a medium bowl, stir together the peppers, eggplant, garlic, and basil until well combined.

TO MAKE THE BURGERS

1. Preheat the grill or a grill pan to high.

2. In a large bowl, use your hands to mix the ground beef, egg, basil, and oregano.

3. Form 8 thin patties of the meat mixture, and place them on a sheet of parchment paper.

4. Use a spoon to gently press down on the center of each patty so that a rim forms around the edge.

5. Add 2 tablespoons of the stuffing to 4 of the patties.

6. Place the 4 additional patties on top of the existing ones. Use your fingers to gently create a seal between the 2 thin patties.

7. Cook the burgers until the sides start to turn brown, then flip to cook the other side until brown. Serve.

FOR THE STUFFING

1 (7-ounce) jar roasted red peppers, drained and finely chopped

1 small eggplant, halved and chopped

2 garlic cloves

½ teaspoon dried basil

FOR THE BURGERS

1½ pounds ground beef

1 egg

1 teaspoon dried basil

1 teaspoon dried oregano

Cooking Tip: *Use a thin, wide spatula to turn the burgers, as they will be very delicate. Don't turn the burgers more than once, as they will be more apt to come unsealed.*

IN MENU FOR WEEK:

 3

PER SERVING:
CALORIES 377
TOTAL FAT 12G
SODIUM 248MG
CARBS 11G
SUGARS 6G
PROTEIN 55G

Taco and Rice Bowl

SERVES 6 / PREP TIME: 10 MINUTES / COOK TIME: 15 MINUTES

2 pounds ground beef

4½ tablespoons Taco Seasoning (page 221)

1 cup water

3 cups Cauliflower Rice (page 150)

1 tomato, diced

Iceberg lettuce, cored and shredded

Cooking Tip: *For some added fun and flavor, top your taco and rice bowl with homemade Guacamole (page 132).*

IN MENU FOR WEEK:

 3

PER SERVING:
CALORIES 509
TOTAL FAT 19G
SODIUM 673MG
CARBS 12G
SUGARS 4G
PROTEIN 72G

Tacos are one of my favorite weeknight meals—hassle-free, and always satisfying. Use my Taco Seasoning (page 221) to make these scrumptious taco bowls, and I guarantee you'll be coming back for more.

1. In a large pan over medium heat, cook the ground beef until fully browned. Reduce the heat to low.

2. Stir in the Taco Seasoning and water. Cook until the seasoning has thickened, stirring regularly.

3. Using a large spoon, put the Cauliflower Rice in serving bowls. Top with the meat mixture, diced tomatoes, and shredded lettuce and serve.

Chili-Lime Flat Iron Steak

SERVES 4 / PREP TIME: 5 MINUTES, PLUS 6 HOURS TO MARINATE / COOK TIME: 10 MINUTES

I love a good steak almost more than my morning cup of coffee. This recipe is one of my favorites, as the steak marinates all day in a mouthwatering sauce and is ready to toss on the grill when you get home. I especially enjoy the incredible flavor contrast of spice and citrus produced by the marinade's chili and lime.

1. In a large baking dish or gallon-size resealable bag, add the apple cider vinegar, white vinegar, olive oil, lime juice, cumin, garlic powder, chili powder, oregano, and pepper.

2. Stir or shake well to combine all ingredients.

3. Add the steak to the marinade. Seal the bag, or cover the baking dish with plastic wrap.

4. Let the steak sit in the marinade for at least 6 hours.

5. Heat the grill or a grill pan to medium high.

6. Sear the meat on both sides until it is fully cooked and serve.

¼ cup apple cider vinegar

¼ cup white vinegar

½ cup extra-virgin olive oil

Juice of 1 lime

2 tablespoons cumin

¾ teaspoon garlic powder

1 tablespoon chili powder

1 tablespoon dried oregano

1 tablespoon freshly ground black pepper

2 pounds flat iron steak

IN MENU FOR WEEK:

1

PER SERVING:
CALORIES 754
TOTAL FAT 49G
SODIUM 188MG
CARBS 5G
SUGARS 1G
PROTEIN 72G

Tangy Tomato Sirloin Tips

SERVES 4 / PREP TIME: 5 MINUTES / COOK TIME: 35 MINUTES

1½ pounds beef sirloin tips

3 tablespoons extra-virgin olive oil

3 cloves garlic, minced

1 teaspoon onion powder

1 (8-ounce) can tomato sauce

1 cup red wine

2 bay leaves

Sea salt

Freshly ground black pepper

IN MENU FOR WEEK:

PER SERVING:
CALORIES 384
TOTAL FAT 18G
SODIUM 465MG
CARBS 6G
SUGARS 3G
PROTEIN 37G

I know what you're thinking: "Tomato sauce with steak?" Give these a try, and you won't regret it. The tangy tomato and wine combination gives this beef an out-of-this-world flavor.

1. Using a sharp knife, cut the beef tips into equal-size cubes.

2. In a large skillet over medium-high heat, heat the olive oil.

3. Add the garlic and onion powder, and sauté until the garlic is tender.

4. Place the beef cubes in the skillet, and cook until browned.

5. Reduce the heat to low. Add the tomato sauce, red wine, and bay leaves to the pan.

6. Season with salt and pepper.

7. Cook for 30 minutes, stirring often to ensure the sauce does not stick, and serve.

Herb Meatballs

SERVES 4 / PREP TIME: 5 MINUTES / COOK TIME: 25 MINUTES

Making meatballs used to be a full-day affair in my house. The meatballs would cook all day in a big pot of sauce, and we would enjoy them with a big spaghetti dinner. Unfortunately there's just no time for that during the week, so I created this recipe. Packed with flavor but ready in much less time, these meatballs are sensational over a pile of vegetable pasta.

1. Preheat the oven to 350°F.
2. In a large bowl, use your hands to mix the ground beef, spinach, garlic, almond meal, eggs, onion powder, oregano, basil, and parsley, and season with salt and pepper.
3. Line a baking sheet with parchment paper.
4. Form meatballs the size of ping-pong balls, and place them on the baking sheet.
5. Bake until the meatballs are brown, about 25 minutes, and serve.

1 pound ground beef

1 cup spinach, minced

4 garlic cloves, minced

½ cup almond meal

4 eggs

1 teaspoon onion powder

1 tablespoon oregano

1 tablespoon dried basil

1 tablespoon dried parsley

Sea salt

Freshly ground
  black pepper

IN MENU FOR WEEK:

4

PER SERVING:
CALORIES 355
TOTAL FAT 18G
SODIUM 202MG
CARBS 5G
SUGARS 1G
PROTEIN 43G

Carne Asada with Chimichurri

SERVES 6 / PREP TIME: 10 MINUTES, PLUS 2½ HOURS TO MARINATE / COOK TIME: 10 MINUTES

2 pounds rib eye steak

Juice of 1 lime

3 garlic cloves, minced

1 tablespoon chili powder

1 tablespoon paprika

1½ teaspoons dried oregano

½ teaspoon cumin

½ teaspoon chipotle chili powder

Sea salt

Freshly ground black pepper

1 tablespoon grass-fed butter

Chimichurri (page 229)

IN MENU FOR WEEK:

 3

PER SERVING:
CALORIES 351
TOTAL FAT 18G
SODIUM 1812MG
CARBS 3G
SUGARS 0G
PROTEIN 42G

You know the saying: "Good things come to those who wait"? That's definitely the case with my carne asada recipe! Due to the time required for marinating, you'll probably want to prep this in advance, but the perfectly paired spices mixed with fresh Chimichurri will be so worth it.

1. Place the steak on a cutting board, and pour the lime juice over it to coat completely. Rub the lime juice into the meat.

2. In a small bowl, mix together the garlic, chili powder, paprika, oregano, cumin, and chipotle chili powder, salt, and pepper.

3. Rub the dry seasonings into the meat, place it in a plastic bag or on a plate covered with plastic wrap, and refrigerate for 2 hours.

4. Remove the meat from the refrigerator, and allow it to come to room temperature for 30 minutes.

5. In a large skillet over medium-high heat, melt the butter.

6. Place the steak in the skillet, and sear for 4 minutes on each side.

7. Plate, top with Chimichurri, and serve.

Baked Spaghetti Bolognese

SERVES 6 / PREP TIME: 10 MINUTES / COOK TIME: 1 HOUR 25 MINUTES

1 large spaghetti squash

1 pound ground beef

1 cup baby spinach,
  coarsely chopped

2 cups tomato sauce

1 teaspoon dried basil

½ teaspoon dried oregano

3 eggs

IN MENU FOR WEEK:

PER SERVING:
CALORIES 224
TOTAL FAT 8G
SODIUM 530MG
CARBS 12G
SUGARS 4G
PROTEIN 28G

I struggled with naming this dish for a long time. It's not quite lasagna, but not quite a Bolognese, so this title combining the two was the only one that seemed appropriate. This dish bakes together all of my favorite Italian flavors into one bite—but feel free to add your favorites, as well. I'm sure it would be delicious with sausage and pepperoni.

1. Preheat the oven to 425°F.

2. Halve the spaghetti squash lengthwise.

3. Using a large spoon, scrape out all the seeds and loose fibers from each half.

4. Line a baking sheet with aluminum foil.

5. Place the spaghetti squash face down on the baking sheet, and bake for 25 minutes.

6. While the squash is cooking, in a medium pan over medium heat, cook the ground beef until browned.

7. Add the baby spinach, tomato sauce, basil, and oregano. Turn to low and simmer.

8. Remove the squash from the oven, and turn the halves over so they are face up. Allow them to cool for 5 minutes. Reduce the oven heat to 350°F.

9. Scrape the insides of the squash halves with a large fork to create "spaghetti" strands. Put the spaghetti in a 9-by-13-inch glass or ceramic baking dish.

10. In a small bowl, whisk the eggs, and add them to the baking dish.

11. Pour the meat and tomato sauce mixture into the baking dish, and carefully stir to combine all ingredients.

12. Place the baking dish in the oven, and bake for 1 hour.

13. Allow the dish to cool for 10 minutes. Cut into squares using the edge of a spatula and serve.

Easy Meatloaf

SERVES 6 / PREP TIME: 5 MINUTES / COOK TIME: 60 MINUTES

2 pounds ground beef

1 cup almond meal

2 eggs

**1 (6-ounce) can
tomato paste**

3 garlic cloves, minced

2 tablespoons dried basil

1½ teaspoons sea salt

1 teaspoon dried oregano

1 teaspoon onion powder

**Freshly ground
black pepper**

IN MENU FOR WEEK:

 2

PER SERVING:
CALORIES 421
TOTAL FAT 19G
SODIUM 617MG
CARBS 10G
SUGARS 4G
PROTEIN 53G

At an early age I swore off meatloaf all together. I just couldn't get behind it. Well, let me warn you, this isn't your mother's meatloaf. This one is made with all fresh ingredients, almond flour, and no ketchup. I'm happy to say meatloaf and I have made up.

1. Preheat the oven to 350°F.

2. In a large bowl, use your hands to mix together the ground beef, almond meal, eggs, tomato paste, garlic, basil, salt, oregano, onion powder, and pepper until the mixture is consistent throughout.

3. In a large glass baking pan or bread loaf pan, form the meat mixture into a rectangular loaf.

4. Bake for 1 hour, until the center is no longer pink, and serve.

Mom's Pot Roast

SERVES 6 / PREP TIME: 10 MINUTES / COOK TIME: 4 TO 7 HOURS

Pot roast is always a crowd pleaser, but finding the perfect recipe takes a lot of trial and error. This recipe is foolproof and lets the slow cooker do all the work. You'll come home to a perfectly cooked roast and a house that smells like heaven.

1. Place the chuck roast in a slow cooker, and season with salt and pepper.
2. Add the garlic, red onion, and carrots on top of the roast.
3. Pour in the beef broth and red wine (if using) to surround the roast.
4. Cook on high for 4 hours or low for 7 hours and serve.

3 pounds chuck roast

Sea salt

Freshly ground black pepper

3 garlic cloves, minced

½ cup red onion, coarsely chopped

1½ cups carrots, coarsely chopped

2½ cups beef broth

1 cup red wine (optional)

Cooking Tip: *Feel free to switch up the vegetables based on what you have available. I like to add sweet potatoes, celery, and mushrooms when I have them on hand. Although all the alcohol will cook off, you can also leave out the red wine if you prefer.*

IN MENU FOR WEEK:

2

PER SERVING:
CALORIES 556
TOTAL FAT 19G
SODIUM 528MG
CARBS 6G
SUGARS 2G
PROTEIN 77G

DESSERTS

Berries and Coconut Whip

SERVES 4 / PREP TIME: 5 MINUTES

2 cups mixed berries

1 (13½-ounce) can full-fat coconut milk, chilled

½ teaspoon vanilla extract

1 teaspoon honey

PER SERVING:
CALORIES 223
TOTAL FAT 18G
SODIUM 22MG
CARBS 13G
SUGARS 8G
PROTEIN 2G

A family favorite for all holidays, Berries and Coconut Whip is the perfect dessert year round. Use in-season berries, and top them with this simple coconut whip. Not only is this recipe delicious, but it's light enough to eat after a meal without feeling guilty.

1. Rinse the berries and set them aside on a paper towel to dry.

2. Take the chilled can of coconut milk from the fridge. The solids will rise to the top.

3. Turn the can upside down, open the bottom, and pour out the liquid.

4. Scoop the hardened coconut cream into a bowl, and use an electric hand mixer to whip it.

5. Add the vanilla extract and honey to the coconut cream, and whip it again until creamy.

6. Place a scoop (½ cup) of berries into each of 4 bowls, top each with a generous portion of coconut whip, and serve.

Chocolate-Covered Coconut Bites

SERVES 6 TO 8 / PREP TIME: 10 MINUTES, PLUS 35 MINUTES FOR FREEZING / COOK TIME: 5 MINUTES

Make a batch of these tasty little candies, and keep them in the back of your fridge for emergencies. Perfectly bite-size, these will relieve your sugar craving without pushing you off track.

1. In a large bowl, whisk together the maple syrup, 4 tablespoons of coconut oil, and the vanilla extract.

2. Slowly add the shredded coconut while continuously stirring.

3. Roll the coconut mixture into round balls, and arrange them on a parchment paper–lined baking sheet.

4. Place the baking sheet in the freezer for 30 minutes, or until the coconut balls are firm to the touch.

5. Place the dark chocolate chips and remaining tablespoon of coconut oil in a microwaveable bowl, and microwave for 4 to 5 minutes, stirring frequently, until melted.

6. Remove the coconut balls from the freezer, and coat them in melted chocolate.

7. Place each chocolate-covered coconut ball back on the lined baking sheet, and place the baking sheet back in the freezer until the chocolate hardens and serve.

3 tablespoons maple syrup

5 tablespoons coconut oil, divided

1 teaspoon vanilla extract

2 cups unsweetened finely shredded coconut

1 cup dark chocolate chips

Cooking Tip: *To achieve the right coconut consistency, it is important to use finely shredded coconut. If this option is not available at your local market, buy regular unsweetened coconut flakes and use a food processor to grind the coconut to the correct consistency.*

PER SERVING:
CALORIES 415
TOTAL FAT 177G
SODIUM 10MG
CARBS 27G
SUGARS 19G
PROTEIN 3G

Dark Chocolate Pudding

SERVES 4 / PREP TIME: 5 MINUTES / COOK TIME: 15 MINUTES

1 (13½-ounce) can coconut milk

2 egg yolks

½ cup dark chocolate chips

1 teaspoon vanilla extract

1 tablespoon honey

Cooking Tip: *This pudding is thick, so when filling your serving dishes, make sure to spread the pudding evenly and compactly to avoid air pockets.*

PER SERVING:
CALORIES 336
TOTAL FAT 29G
SODIUM 19MG
CARBS 20G
SUGARS 16G
PROTEIN 5G

Rich and creamy, this decadent, dark chocolate pudding is far better than the boxed stuff your mom used to make. Top the pudding with Coconut Whip (page 206) for a little added flair.

1. In a medium pot over medium heat, heat the coconut milk and egg yolks, stirring continuously.

2. Remove the pot from the heat, and stir in the dark chocolate chips, vanilla extract, and honey until smooth.

3. Transfer the pudding to individual dishes and chill for 2 hours, or until it sets, and serve.

Fudge Brownies

SERVES 15 / PREP TIME: 5 MINUTES / COOK TIME: 30 MINUTES

When it comes to brownies, my mantra is the fudgier the better. That's why my goal was not just to create the best Paleo fudge brownies around, but the best fudge brownies ever. I think I succeeded.

1. Preheat the oven to 300°F.
2. In a large bowl, mix the coconut flour, cacao powder, butter, eggs, and maple syrup until well combined.
3. Grease a baking dish with coconut oil, and pour the brownie batter into the baking dish.
4. Bake for 30 minutes, or until a toothpick comes out clean, and serve.

¼ cup plus 3 tablespoons coconut flour

½ cup cacao powder

½ cup plus 2 tablespoons grass-fed butter, melted

3 eggs

½ cup plus 2 tablespoons maple syrup

Coconut oil, for greasing

PER SERVING:
CALORIES 97
TOTAL FAT 5G
SODIUM 42MG
CARBS 13G
SUGARS 9G
PROTEIN 3G

Coconut Macaroons

SERVES 8 TO 10 / PREP TIME: 10 MINUTES / COOK TIME: 15 MINUTES

5 large egg whites

¼ cup honey

2 cups unsweetened shredded coconut

1 teaspoon vanilla extract

Dash Himalayan sea salt

Cooking Tip: *If you have a sweet tooth, melt ½ cup of chocolate chips, and dip the bottom of the macaroons in the melted chocolate.*

PER SERVING:
CALORIES 224
TOTAL FAT 16G
SODIUM 62MG
CARBS 15G
SUGARS 11G
PROTEIN 4G

Coconut macaroons are some of the easiest cookies to make. These little bites are light and sweet, with just the perfect amount of coconut flavor. For a bit of variety, add a handful of dark chocolate chips, raisins, cranberries, or nuts.

1. Preheat the oven to 350°F.
2. In a large bowl, whisk together the egg whites and honey until fluffy.
3. Add the coconut, vanilla, and salt to the bowl, and mix well.
4. Spoon out 1-teaspoon balls of the coconut mixture onto a parchment paper–lined baking sheet.
5. Bake for 12 to 15 minutes, until lightly golden brown, and serve.

Almond Butter Bars

SERVES 12 / PREP TIME: 20 MINUTES, PLUS 2 HOURS FOR FREEZING

¾ cup almond flour

½ cup unsweetened
   shredded coconut

¾ cup coconut sugar

1 cup almond butter

4 tablespoons
   coconut oil, divided

1 cup dark chocolate chips

PER SERVING:
CALORIES 338
TOTAL FAT 25G
SODIUM 2MG
CARBS 25G
SUGARS 18G
PROTEIN 5G

No need to turn the oven on for this recipe. In fact, this recipe is completely stove free. All you need is a microwave and freezer to make these easy Almond Butter Bars. If you prefer, you can also substitute the almond butter with sunflower butter or another nut butter of your choice.

1. In a large bowl, stir together the almond flour, shredded coconut, and coconut sugar.

2. In a microwavable bowl, heat the almond butter and 2 tablespoons of coconut oil until melted, stirring occasionally.

3. Remove the almond butter from the microwave, and add to the dry ingredients. Mix until well combined.

4. Lightly grease a baking dish with 1 tablespoon of coconut oil.

5. Press the batter into the baking dish.

6. In a microwavable bowl, cook the dark chocolate chips and remaining tablespoon of coconut oil for 4 to 5 minutes, stirring frequently, until melted.

7. Pour the chocolate over the almond butter mixture, and smooth evenly.

8. Freeze for 2 hours, remove, slice into 12 squares, and serve.

Strawberry Ice Cream

SERVES 4 / PREP TIME: 10 MINUTES, PLUS 25 HOURS 30 MINUTES FOR FREEZING

There is something about a warm summer afternoon that makes a cold, sweet treat extra enjoyable, but you don't have to cave into sugary ice pops or heavy ice creams to get your frozen dessert fix. This recipe for strawberry ice cream is delicious, nutritious, and the perfect way to cool down.

1. In a blender, blend the coconut milk, frozen strawberries, honey, and vanilla until smooth.

2. Pour the mixture into a freezer-safe bowl or loaf pan, and freeze for 30 minutes.

3. Remove from the freezer and whisk vigorously.

4. Refreeze the ice cream mixture, continuing to whisk every 30 minutes 4 more times.

5. Freeze overnight and serve.

1 (13½-ounce) can full-fat coconut milk
½ cup frozen strawberries
⅓ cup honey
1 teaspoon vanilla extract

Cooking Tip: *Use this recipe method to make all your favorite ice cream flavors. Replace the strawberries with any frozen fruit, or sub out the fruit altogether for nut butter and dark chocolate chips.*

PER SERVING:
CALORIES 282
TOTAL FAT 18G
SODIUM 23MG
CARBS 31G
SUGARS 29G
PROTEIN 2G

Blueberry Crisp

SERVES 4 / PREP TIME: 10 MINUTES / COOK TIME: 15 MINUTES

Fruit crisps are always a quick and delicious dessert. The best part is you can make them with just about any fruit you have in the house—I like to use berries in the summer but switch them out for apples in the fall.

1. Preheat the oven to 350°F.

2. Rinse the berries, and set them aside on a paper towel to dry.

3. In a small bowl, mix together the almond flour, almond butter, maple syrup, vanilla, cinnamon, and salt until a crumble forms.

4. In a large bowl, stir together the blueberries and coconut oil until well coated.

5. Pour the blueberries into a baking dish and spread evenly. Top the blueberries with the almond flour mixture.

6. Bake for 15 to 20 minutes, or until the topping begins to turn golden brown, and serve.

1 pint fresh blueberries

¼ cup almond flour

3 tablespoons almond butter

1 tablespoon maple syrup

1 teaspoon vanilla extract

1 teaspoon cinnamon

⅛ teaspoon sea salt

1½ tablespoons coconut oil, melted

Make-Ahead Tip: *If you are hosting a dinner party, you can make this recipe in the morning and keep it in the fridge until guests arrive. When you sit down to dinner, pop it in the oven, and it will be hot and crisp by the time you're ready for dessert.*

PER SERVING:
CALORIES 240
TOTAL FAT 16G
SODIUM 60MG
CARBS 22G
SUGARS 13G
PROTEIN 3G

Roasted Peaches
with Pecans and Honey

SERVES 4 / PREP TIME: 5 MINUTES / COOK TIME: 30 MINUTES

**2 large, ripe peaches,
halved and pitted**

¼ teaspoon cinnamon

2 teaspoons honey

¼ cup crushed pecans

PER SERVING:
CALORIES 94
TOTAL FAT 6G
SODIUM 0MG
CARBS 12G
SUGARS 10G
PROTEIN 2G

In late summer, when fruit reaches its peak, let peaches be the star of your dessert. Roast the fruit in the oven to bring out its sweet and succulent flavors.

1. Preheat the oven to 350°F.

2. Place the peaches on a baking sheet cut-side up.

3. Sprinkle with cinnamon, top with pecans, and drizzle ½ teaspoon of honey over each half.

4. Bake in the oven for 30 minutes and serve.

Toasted Bananas

SERVES 1 / PREP TIME: 5 MINUTES / COOK TIME: 4 MINUTES

Caramelized bananas are a quick dessert to prepare—and much simpler than you may think. Enjoy them on their own as a midnight snack, or as a unique topping over your favorite grain-free cake.

1. In a small bowl, whisk together the honey and water.
2. Heat a small pan over medium heat, and grease using coconut oil.
3. Add the bananas to the pan in one layer, and cook for 1 to 2 minutes on each side.
4. Remove the pan from the heat, and add the honey mixture. Sprinkle with cinnamon and serve.

1 tablespoon honey

1 tablespoon water

Coconut oil, for greasing

1 banana, sliced

Cinnamon, for sprinkling

PER SERVING:
CALORIES 188
TOTAL FAT 3G
SODIUM 2MG
CARBS 44G
SUGARS 32G
PROTEIN 1G

KITCHEN STAPLES

Steak Rub

MAKES 1¼ CUPS / PREP TIME: 5 MINUTES

⅓ cup sea salt

¼ cup coconut sugar

¼ cup paprika

2 tablespoons dried oregano

2 tablespoons dried thyme

2 tablespoons freshly
  ground black pepper

1 tablespoon
  cayenne pepper

Cooking Tip: *If the cayenne pepper is too hot for your taste, start with ½ teaspoon and add more until you reach your desired heat level.*

PER SERVING (2 TABLESPOONS):
CALORIES 34
TOTAL FAT 1G
SODIUM 3372MG
CARBS 8G
SUGARS 5G
PROTEIN 1G

This combination of herbs and spices will give any cut of steak a burst of flavor, turning even the most novice cook into a grill master.

1. In a medium bowl, stir together the salt, coconut sugar, paprika, oregano, thyme, black pepper, and cayenne pepper until thoroughly combined.

2. Use immediately, or store in an airtight bag or container for up to 30 days.

Taco Seasoning

MAKES ¼ CUP / PREP TIME: 5 MINUTES

Tacos are a quick and easy meal that can be made in a matter of minutes. This versatile mix can be added to ground beef, chicken, or fish, and it is significantly more flavorful than the packaged mix at your local market.

1. In a small bowl, stir together the chili powder, cumin, paprika, onion powder, garlic salt, and salt until thoroughly combined.

2. Use immediately, or store in an airtight bag or container for up to 30 days.

4 teaspoons chili powder

1 tablespoon cumin

1 tablespoon paprika

2 teaspoons onion powder

1½ teaspoons garlic salt

1 teaspoon sea salt

Cooking Tip: *For best results, use 2 tablespoons of mix mixed with ¼ cup of water per 1 pound of meat.*

PER SERVING (1 TABLESPOON):
CALORIES 26
TOTAL FAT 1G
SODIUM 498MG
CARBS 5G
SUGARS 1G
PROTEIN 1G

Burger Seasoning

MAKES ½ CUP / PREP TIME: 5 MINUTES

5 teaspoons paprika

4 teaspoons sea salt

4 teaspoons garlic powder

2 teaspoons onion powder

1½ teaspoons freshly
  ground black pepper

1 teaspoon white pepper

½ teaspoon cayenne pepper

Cooking Tip: *Use 1 tablespoon of burger seasoning
per 1 pound of meat.*

PER SERVING (1 TABLESPOON):
CALORIES 13
TOTAL FAT 0G
SODIUM 937MG
CARBS 3G
SUGARS 1G
PROTEIN 1G

*Whether you are hosting a summer barbecue or just looking to
spice up your weeknight burger, this seasoning will have everyone
asking for seconds.*

1. In a small bowl, stir together the paprika, salt, garlic
   powder, onion powder, pepper, white pepper, and
   cayenne pepper until thoroughly combined.

2. Use immediately, or store in an airtight bag or container
   for up to 30 days.

Ranch Seasoning

MAKES ⅓ CUP / PREP TIME: 5 MINUTES

This recipe is terrifically versatile. It's excellent for flavoring grilled chicken and pairs perfectly with Buffalo wings as a dipping sauce.

1. In a small bowl, stir together the dried parsley, onion powder, garlic powder, dill weed, dried chives, salt, and pepper until thoroughly combined.

2. Use immediately, or store in an airtight bag or container for up to 30 days.

2 tablespoons dried parsley

1 tablespoon onion powder

2 teaspoons garlic powder

1½ teaspoons dill weed

1 teaspoon dried chives

1 teaspoon sea salt

1 teaspoon freshly ground black pepper

Cooking Tip: *Looking for a quick and easy, light Ranch Dressing? Combine 1 tablespoon of this homemade Ranch Seasoning with ⅓ cup Mayonnaise (page 230) and ⅓ cup coconut milk. Whisk together until smooth.*

PER SERVING (1 TABLESPOON):
CALORIES 9
TOTAL FAT 0G
SODIUM 314MG
CARBS 2G
SUGARS 1G
PROTEIN 0G

Garlic Aioli

MAKES 1 CUP / PREP TIME: 10 MINUTES

½ cup Mayonnaise
(page 230)

3 garlic cloves, minced

2½ tablespoons freshly
squeezed lemon juice

¾ teaspoon sea salt

½ teaspoon freshly ground
black pepper

PER SERVING:
CALORIES 67
TOTAL FAT 7G
SODIUM 142MG
CARBS 0G
SUGARS 0G
PROTEIN 1G

This recipe is one of my all-time favorites. When we have friends over to watch a football game, you can bet I am serving a pile of sweet potato fries with a side of this homemade Garlic Aioli!

1. In a blender, blend the Mayonnaise, garlic, lemon juice, salt, and pepper on low until well combined.

2. Use immediately, or cover and refrigerate for up to 7 days.

Simple Lemon Dressing

MAKES 1 CUP / PREP TIME: 10 MINUTES

4 tablespoons freshly
  squeezed lemon juice

2 tablespoon Dijon mustard

2 teaspoons shallot,
  finely minced

2 garlic cloves, minced

½ cup extra-virgin olive oil

Sea salt

Freshly ground
  black pepper

PER SERVING (2 TABLESPOONS):
CALORIES 114
TOTAL FAT 13G
SODIUM 77MG
CARBS 1G
SUGARS 0G
PROTEIN 0G

This simple lemon dressing is a staple in our house. It complements just about every salad combination you can think up, and adds delicate citrus flavor when drizzled over a simple chicken dish.

1. In a medium bowl, whisk the lemon juice, Dijon mustard, shallot, and garlic until well combined.

2. Slowly add the olive oil, while continuing to whisk until the dressing has thickened.

3. Season with salt and pepper and serve.

Spiced Cider Vinaigrette

MAKES 1 CUP / PREP TIME: 10 MINUTES

When out to eat, oil and vinegar is an easy choice for a simple, clean salad dressing. However, when we are home, I like to spice things up a bit. This vinaigrette is one of my favorites, and it works just as well over a simple green salad as over one more complex, such as an Apple Walnut Vegetable Salad (page 106).

1. In a medium bowl, whisk the apple juice, apple cider vinegar, honey, salt, and pepper until well combined.
2. Slowly add the olive oil, while continuing to whisk until the dressing has thickened, and serve.

1 cup apple juice

4 tablespoons apple cider vinegar

2 tablespoons honey

½ teaspoon sea salt

¼ teaspoon freshly ground black pepper

¼ cup extra-virgin olive oil

PER SERVING (2 TABLESPOONS):
CALORIES 86
TOTAL FAT 6G
SODIUM 119MG
CARBS 8G
SUGARS 8G
PROTEIN 0G

Chimichurri

MAKES 2 CUPS / PREP TIME: 5 MINUTES

There are so many cuts of steak to choose from at your local grocery store or butcher shop. If you're looking to try something new, add this quick and flavorful Chimichurri to your dish the next time you're dining on a nice piece of meat.

1. In a blender, blend the parsley, olive oil, red wine vinegar, cilantro, garlic, crushed red pepper, cumin, and salt on medium for 10 seconds.
2. Scrape down the sides of the blender pitcher to reincorporate the mixture.
3. Blend on medium for 20 seconds, or until all ingredients are fully combined.
4. Use immediately, or within 2 hours of preparation.

2 cups fresh Italian parsley

1 cup extra-virgin olive oil

⅔ cup red wine vinegar

¼ cup fresh cilantro

4 garlic cloves, peeled

1½ teaspoons dried crushed red pepper

1 teaspoon cumin

¾ teaspoon sea salt

PER SERVING (¼ CUP):
CALORIES 231
TOTAL FAT 25G
SODIUM 186MG
CARBS 2G
SUGARS 0G
PROTEIN 1G

Mayonnaise

MAKES 1½ CUPS / PREP TIME: 5 MINUTES

2 eggs

1 cup extra-virgin olive oil

Juice of 1 lemon

Sea salt

Cooking Tip: *Impress your guests with fancy flavors, like chipotle or roasted garlic, by adding herbs and spices. Experiment and have fun with it.*

PER SERVING (2
TABLESPOONS):
CALORIES 154
TOTAL FAT 18G
SODIUM 30MG
CARBS 0G
SUGARS 0G
PROTEIN 1G

Homemade mayonnaise is incredibly easy to make, and it provides a healthy alternative to store-bought versions filled with additives and preservatives.

1. In a blender, blend the eggs, olive oil, lemon juice, and salt on medium to high until smooth, about 20 seconds.

2. Use immediately, or cover and refrigerate for up to 4 days.

Ketchup

MAKES 2 CUPS / PREP TIME: 5 MINUTES / COOK TIME: 10 MINUTES

This recipe boasts the same tomato taste without all the sugar, additives, and preservatives found in store-bought ketchup. I used to think that making homemade condiments would be difficult and time consuming, but you can easily prep this recipe in advance, and keep a bottle in your fridge for later use.

1. In a blender, blend the tomato paste, ⅓ of cup water, the apple cider vinegar, and the honey on medium until well combined.

2. In a medium saucepan over medium heat, cook the mixture for 5 minutes.

3. Add the garlic powder, onion powder, nutmeg, cloves, pepper, and remaining tablespoon of water to the mixture, and season with salt.

4. Cook the mixture over low heat for 5 minutes, stirring constantly.

5. Cool and serve, or refrigerate in an airtight container for up to 7 days.

1 (6-ounce) can tomato paste

⅓ cup plus 1 tablespoon water, divided

1 tablespoon apple cider vinegar

½ teaspoon honey

2 teaspoons garlic powder

1½ teaspoons onion powder

½ teaspoon nutmeg

½ teaspoon cloves

¼ teaspoon freshly ground black pepper

Sea salt

PER SERVING (2 TABLESPOONS):
CALORIES 12
TOTAL FAT 0G
SODIUM 26MG
CARBS 3G
SUGARS 2G
PROTEIN 1G

Applesauce

SERVES 4 TO 6 / PREP TIME: 15 MINUTES / COOK TIME: 20 MINUTES

¾ cup water

6 apples, peeled, cored, and diced

2 tablespoons honey

¼ teaspoon cinnamon

Cooking Tip: *Applesauce can be canned and stored year round, or you can simply freeze it using freezer-safe storage containers.*

IN MENU FOR WEEKS:

 2 3

PER SERVING:
CALORIES 174
TOTAL FAT 1G
SODIUM 3MG
CARBS 47G
SUGARS 37G
PROTEIN 1G

Every fall we go apple picking and come home with more apples than we know what to do with. After we make the obligatory apple crisp and apple cider donuts, I cook down the leftovers into applesauce that will last the rest of the year. This Applesauce is not only a flavorful side dish, but it can be used in a number of your favorite baked goods.

1. In a medium pot over medium-high heat, heat the water.
2. Add the apples, honey, and cinnamon to the water, and stir.
3. Cover and cook for 15 to 20 minutes, or until the apples cook down and are soft, stirring occasionally.
4. Remove the pot from the heat, and mash until the apples reach the desired consistency.
5. Scoop the applesauce into a storage container, place in the refrigerator until chilled, and serve.

Mustard

½ cup dry mustard

½ cup water

Sea salt

PER SERVING (1 TABLESPOON):
CALORIES 46
TOTAL FAT 3G
SODIUM 32MG
CARBS 4G
SUGARS 1G
PROTEIN 3G

I used to think mustard was only for hot dogs, but now that I have become more adventurous in the kitchen, I have found a number of ways to incorporate it into my recipes. This recipe is ridiculously simple and takes less than five minutes.

1. In a small bowl, whisk together the dry mustard, water, and salt until fully combined.

2. Let the mixture sit for 15 minutes before using, or cover and refrigerate for up to 7 days.

Honey Mustard

MAKES ½ CUP / PREP TIME: 5 MINUTES

The great thing about honey mustard is that it can be used either as a condiment for dipping snacks or as a dressing for a quick side salad. This recipe uses the natural sweetness of maple syrup to kick the store-bought version right to the curb.

1. In a small bowl, whisk together the olive oil, Dijon mustard, maple syrup, and pepper until well combined.

2. Use immediately, or cover and refrigerate for up to 7 days.

3 tablespoons extra-virgin olive oil

3 tablespoons Dijon mustard

1 tablespoon maple syrup

Freshly ground black pepper

PER SERVING (1 TABLESPOON):
CALORIES 56
TOTAL FAT 6G
SODIUM 67MG
CARBS 2G
SUGARS 2G
PROTEIN 0G

Salsa

MAKES 2 CUPS / PREP TIME: 10 MINUTES

3 tomatoes, diced

½ onion, chopped

1 jalapeño, chopped

Juice of 1 lime

1 tablespoon extra-virgin
  olive oil

Fresh cilantro, chopped

Sea salt

With fresh ingredients and bold flavors, you'll never go back to store-bought salsa once you taste this homemade alternative.

1. In a large bowl, stir together the tomatoes, onion, and jalapeño.

2. Add the lime juice and olive oil, and stir until the mixture has an even consistency.

3. Top the salsa with fresh cilantro, season with salt, and serve.

IN MENU FOR WEEKS:

PER SERVING (¼ CUP):
CALORIES 27
TOTAL FAT 2G
SODIUM 34MG
CARBS 3G
SUGARS 2G
PROTEIN 1G

Almond Butter

MAKES 1 CUP / PREP TIME: 5 MINUTES, PLUS 24 HOURS FOR SOAKING / COOK TIME: 30 MINUTES

In my prior life, I lived on peanut butter. Although almond butter is not an exact replica of my childhood favorite, it certainly offers a great alternative. Nut butter can also be paired with fruit for a delicious midday snack.

1. In a medium container, cover the almonds with water; add a dash of salt, and let them soak overnight.

2. Drain the almonds well, and place them on a paper towel to dry.

3. Preheat the oven to 350°F.

4. Line a baking sheet with parchment paper, and lay the almonds on the sheet in a single layer.

5. Roast for 5 minutes.

6. In a food processor, grind the almonds until they become a fine powder.

7. Add the coconut oil to the food processor, and grind for 10 to 15 minutes, stopping to scrape down the sides as needed.

8. Add the maple syrup, and grind for another 10 minutes, stopping to scrape down the sides, until smooth and creamy.

2 cups raw almonds

Dash sea salt

2 tablespoons coconut oil

2 tablespoons maple syrup

IN MENU FOR WEEKS:

 2 3

PER SERVING (1 TABLESPOON):
CALORIES 90
TOTAL FAT 8G
SODIUM 16MG
CARBS 4G
SUGARS 2G
PROTEIN 3G

Acknowledgments

To my mom, Patricia: Thank you for always believing in me and encouraging me to follow my heart and chase my dreams. You taught me that hard work can take you far in this world, and your love and support has meant everything to me. I would not be the woman I am today without you.

To my brothers, Michael and Nickolas: Thank you for giving it to me straight with no sugar coating. I love you more than you know and keep a piece of each of you with me always.

To my grandparents, Joyce and Bob, my loudest cheerleaders and biggest fans: Thank you for supporting me no matter what.

To my boyfriend, Julien: Thank you for constantly having faith in me, even when I did not have enough in myself. This book would never have happened without you and your support for everything I do. You are my rock, my best friend, and my most honest critic. Thank you for taking this journey with me and supporting me along the way. I am so grateful to have you in my life.

To my friends and family, my taste testers and confidants: Thank you for always eating my kitchen experiments, cheering for me throughout this journey, and not once complaining when I hosted a Paleo dinner party or brought a Paleo dessert to an event.

To Sam, for encouraging me to try new things: Without you I would never have found the healthy lifestyle I believe in so strongly. You showed me the Paleo ropes, encouraged me to start a blog, and still inspire me every day.

To Talia and my team at Callisto Media: Thank you for all of your time and patience throughout this entire process, for guiding me along the way, and for your constant encouragement.

Last but definitely not least, to my fabulous readers: Thank you for all of your kind words and continued support. My blog and this book would not exist without each and every one of you. Thank you from the bottom of my heart.

About the Author

Kenzie Swanhart is the founder and author of the popular food blog *Cave Girl in the City*. In an effort to find balance and regain a healthy lifestyle after college, Kenzie adopted the Paleo diet. She started her blog to share her successes, resources, and findings with others on a similar journey. Her goal has always been to help others look and feel their best without feeling deprived.

Kenzie and her boyfriend, Julien, live in Boston with their dog, Charlie.

APPENDIX A

The Clean Fifteen and the Dirty Dozen

Each year, the Environmental Working Group (EWG), an environmental organization based in the United States, publishes a list they call "The Dirty Dozen." These are the fruits and vegetables that, when conventionally grown using chemical pesticides and fertilizers, carry the highest residues. If organically grown isn't an option for you, simply avoid these fruits and vegetables altogether. The list is updated each year, but here is the most recent list (2015).

Similarly, the EWG publishes a list of "The Clean Fifteen," fruits and vegetables that, even when conventionally grown, contain very low levels of chemical pesticide or fertilizer residue. These items are acceptable to purchase conventionally grown.

You might want to snap a photo of these two lists and keep them on your phone to reference while shopping. Or you can download the EWG's app to your phone or tablet.

THE CLEAN FIFTEEN

Asparagus
Avocados
Cabbage
Cantaloupe
Cauliflower
Eggplant
Grapefruit
Honeydew melon
Kiwi
Mangos
Onions
Papayas
Pineapples
Sweet corn
Sweet peas (frozen)

THE DIRTY DOZEN

Apples
Celery
Cherries
Grapes
Nectarines (imported)
Peaches
Pears
Potatoes
Spinach
Strawberries
Sweet bell peppers
Tomatoes

Conversion Tables

Volume Equivalents (Liquid)

US STANDARD	US STANDARD (OUNCES)	METRIC (APPROXIMATE)
2 tablespoons	1 fl. oz.	30 mL
¼ cup	2 fl. oz.	60 mL
½ cup	4 fl. oz.	120 mL
1 cup	8 fl. oz.	240 mL
1½ cups	12 fl. oz.	355 mL
2 cups or 1 pint	16 fl. oz.	475 mL
4 cups or 1 quart	32 fl. oz.	1 L
1 gallon	128 fl. oz.	4 L

Volume Equivalents (Dry)

US STANDARD	METRIC (APPROXIMATE)
⅛ teaspoon	0.5 mL
¼ teaspoon	1 mL
½ teaspoon	2 mL
¾ teaspoon	4 mL
1 teaspoon	5 mL
1 tablespoon	15 mL
¼ cup	59 mL
⅓ cup	79 mL
½ cup	118 mL
⅔ cup	156 mL
¾ cup	177 mL
1 cup	235 mL
2 cups or 1 pint	475 mL
3 cups	700 mL
4 cups or 1 quart	1 L
½ gallon	2 L
1 gallon	4 L

Oven Temperatures

FAHRENHEIT (F)	CELSIUS (C) (APPROXIMATE)
250	120
300	150
325	165
350	180
375	190
400	200
425	220
450	230

Weight Equivalents

US STANDARD	METRIC (APPROXIMATE)
½ ounce	15 g
1 ounce	30 g
2 ounces	60 g
4 ounces	115 g
8 ounces	225 g
12 ounces	340 g
16 ounces or 1 pound	455 g

References

American Heart Association. "Frequently Asked Questions About Sugar." Accessed November 28, 2014. http://www.heart.org/HEARTORG/GettingHealthy/NutritionCenter/HealthyDietGoals/Frequently-Asked-Questions-About-Sugar_UCM_306725_Article.jsp.

American Heart Association. "Sugar 101." Accessed November 28, 2014. http://www.heart.org/HEARTORG/GettingHealthy/NutritionCenter/HealthyEating/Sugar-101_UCM_306024_Article.jsp.

American Heart Association. "Suggested Servings from Each Food Group." Accessed November 28, 2014. http://www.heart.org/HEARTORG/GettingHealthy/NutritionCenter/HealthyEating/Suggested-Servings-from-Each-Food-Group_UCM_318186_Article.jsp.

Cordain, Loren. *The Dietary Cure for Acne*. Fort Collins: Paleo Diet Enterprises, LLC, 2006.

Cordain, Loren. "The Nutritional Characteristics of a Contemporary Diet Based Upon Paleolithic Food Groups." *The American Nutraceutical Association* 5 (2002): 15–24.

Frassetto, L.A., M. Schloetter, M. Mietus-Synder, R.C. Morris, Jr., A. Sebastian. "Metabolic and Physiologic Improvements from Consuming a Paleolithic, Hunter-gatherer Type Diet." *European Journal of Clinical Nutrition* 63, no. 8 (August 2009): 947–55. doi: 10.1038/ejcn.2009.4.

Harvard Medical School. "9 Ways to Boost Your Energy." Accessed December 11, 2014. http://www.health.harvard.edu/healthbeat/HEALTHbeat_060706.htm.

Jönsson, T., Y. Granfeldt, B. Ahrén, U.C. Branell, G. Pålsson, A. Hansson, M. Söderström, S. Lindeberg. "Beneficial Effects of a Paleolithic Diet on Cardiovascular Risk Factors in Type 2 Diabetes: A Randomized Cross-over Pilot Study." *Cardiovascular Diabetology* 16, no. 8 (2009): 35. doi: 10.1186/1475-2840-8-35.

Lindeberg, S., T. Jonsson, Y. Granfeldt, E. Borgstrand, J. Soffman, K. Sjostrom, B. Ahren. "A Palaeolithic Diet Improves Glucose Tolerance More than a Mediterranean-like Diet in Individuals with Ischaemic Heart Disease." *Diabetologia* 50, no. 9 (2007): 1795–1807.

Mellberg, C., S. Sandberg, M. Ryberg, M. Eriksson, S. Brage, C. Larsson, et al. "Long-Term Effects of a Palaeolithic-Type Diet in Obese Postmenopausal Women: A 2-Year Randomized Trial." *European Journal of Clinical Nutrition* 68, no. 3 (March 2014): 350–7. doi:10.1038/ejcn.2013.290.

Roberts, Sue. "Six Primary Nutrients Provided by Vegetables." *Healthy Eating, SFGate*. Accessed November 28, 2014. http://healthyeating.sfgate.com/six-primary-nutrients-provided-vegetables-6514.html.

Ryberg, M., S. Sandberg, C. Mellberg, O. Stegle, B. Lindahl, C. Larsson, J. Hauksson, T. Olsson. "A Palaeolithic-type Diet Causes Strong Tissue-specific Effects on Ectopic Fat Deposition in Obese Postmenopausal Women." *Journal of Internal Medicine* 274, no. 1 (July 2013): 67–76. doi: 10.1111/joim.12048.

Recipe Index

Index